Balloon Flowers and Figures

Balloon Flowers and Figures

©Copyright 2019 by Margie Padgitt
All rights reserved.
First Edition
ISBN: 978-0-9988558-3-7

This book and its contents are copyrighted and are proprietary of Margaret Padgitt. Any unauthorized use, reproduction, or transfer of the contents, in any medium is strictly prohibited.

Contributed photos by other designers are copyrighted by the designers and are reprinted here with permission.

Published by UnXMedia

Printed in the United States of America

This book is a combination of two previously published books and additional material

To contact the author or publisher, please write to
M. Padgitt & Associates
1134 S Pearl Street
Independence, MO 64050
816-833-1602
ympadgitt@yahoo.com

Website: www.balloonedu.com

Many thanks to the following contributors who provided photos and descriptions of their work for this project:

Maggie Brusa — The Balloon Platoon, Worcester, Massachusetts

Christopher Horne — Professional Balloon Decorations, Northampton, England

Johnna Perry— Up Up and Away Balloons & Entertainment, Liberty, Missouri

Graham Rouse— CBA - Rouse International, Columbia, South Carolina

Cheryl A. Rupple— C3 Decorating, Defiance, Ohio

Sandi Masori— Balloon Utopia, San Diego, California

Laura Caldwell — (AKA Annie Banannie) of ACME Balloon Company in Southern California

Acknowledgements

Thanks to my daughters, Maria and Rachel, for their long hours of work and creative ideas which helped our balloon business grow.

Special thanks to my daughter, Maria McKenzie, for proofreading and helping make designs for the book, and thanks to my long-time assistant Tamie Dorsch

Special thanks to Jan Iiams, who was the first person to show me how
to make balloon creations in 1991

Thanks to the many balloon professionals I learned from along the way. You are too numerous to mention, but your ideas are always an inspiration.

Introduction

I got involved in the balloon industry in 1993, when I purchased a balloon store in order to expand my floral business. Within a year, balloons were the bulk of our income, with most of our emphasis on corporate and wedding décor. As soon as I found out about all of the different methods to make balloon flowers we eagerly tried them out. It wasn't as easy as it looked, and that inspired me to write this book so that others could learn the technique faster that I did..

I first learned how to make a balloon flower with the "twisted" method by Marvin Hardy at IBAC in 1991. And Jan Iiams taught me how to make cluster balloon flowers out of round balloons in 1992. I picked up the wired flower technique somewhere along the way from several creative people, then experimented on my own with new designs. Other people who have done wonderful designs with balloon flowers are Marloes Bakker-Marsden, Chris Horne, Graham Rouse, and Johnna Perry. There are many others too numerous to mention, but I thank you all for your inspiration.

I took the wired method and created a witch's dress and a Tucan bird body out of over 200 wired petals in 1995 for an IBAC competition, which was my first attempt at detail work with the wired petal method. Then I developed a new idea in a dream in 1998 to make tiny fairies —one day prior to a Kansas City competition— and won first place for the design. They say the best ideas come while you are sleeping.

Fantasy balloon flowers and figures can be made in a myriad of ways and sizes. We are going to explore some of them here and show you the basic techniques, then you can take these ideas and come up with your own variations. I've already seen some great new ideas in classes I teach for balloon artists. Participants always comes up with something new, and I'm sure you'll create your own unique designs after learning the basics in this book.. I hope you find this book helpful.

Sincerely,

Margie Kithcart-Padgitt

Table of Contents

Section I—Fantasy Balloon Flowers	8
History of Fantasy Balloon Flowers	9
Design	11
Tools and Supplies Needed for Construction of Flowers	14
How to Make a Cluster Flower	16
Flower Arch	19
Use of Cluster Flowers in Design	20
Stage Backdrops using Cluster Flowers	22
Twisted Flowers	25
The Easy 8-petal flower	26
The Easy 6-petal flower	28
Flower Stems and Stamens	31
Flower Arrangements	33
Extras to go with Flower Arrangements	38
A Distortion Technique by Graham Rouse	40
More Extras	44
Design Applications	46
Section II—Wired Fantasy Balloon Flowers	47
Wired Fantasy Flower Technique	49
Wired Flower Samples	52
Orchid, Iris, Clusters	53
Inspiration From Nature	54
Wedding Flowers	56
Cake Topper	57
Bird Cage Flowers with no wire	58
Calla Lilly	59
A Lovely Wedding Bouquet	60
Wedding Flower Arrangement, Camellia	62
Ideas for Fantasy Balloon Wedding Flowers	63
Valentine Flowers	64
Retail and Décor Flowers	67
The Three-Colored Flower	68

Holiday Flowers—Poinsettias	69
More Wired Flowers	70
Squiggled and Such	72
More Extra Touches	71
Section II—Fantasy Figures	**75**
Introduction	76
Tools and Supplies needed for construction of Figures	77
The Method: Head, Arms, Legs, and Body	80
Fairy Wings	85
Making Clothing	86
A Jamaican Lady's Dress	88
Clothing for Elves	89
Fabric Clothing	90
Balloon Figure Hair	92
Fairy Hat and Headgear	91
Petal Dress Doll—Alice	95
Fairy with Petal Dress	96
A Woodland Elf	97
A Balloon Ballerina	98
Fantasy Balloon Angel	100
Circus Figures: Clown,, Lion	105
Bar Mitzvah Figures	111
Sushi Bar	112
Balloon Mermaid	113
Balloon Seahorse	114
Centerpiece/Buffet Arrangement	115
Fairies	116
Figures Made with Balloons and Other Materials	117
A Lovely Bride	120
Section III—Balloon Resources	**122**
Glossary of Terms and Balloonisms	123
Resources	126
Books by Margie Padgitt	128
About the Author	129

Section I

Fantasy Balloon Flowers

Cluster flowers, twisted flowers, wired flowers

The History of Fantasy Balloon Flowers

Just what is a Fantasy Balloon Flower anyway? Well, besides the obvious— a flower made out of balloons—a fantasy flower captures the attention of the admirer. It is something unique and different, and is appropriate to use in many different designs, and for events from whimsical to formal.

Suffice it to say that there are many imaginative people that have been making and modifying fantasy flowers for a long time. The term "Fantasy Flowers" was coined in 1983 by Graham Rouse, when he came up with the idea of putting wire inside of balloon stems.

The following information is from Graham Rouse: Graham told me that this may or may not be completely accurate, as other people might remember things differently. Below is a chronology that lists some relevant activities of three key players from the first seven years of Fantasy Flowers. They are Ken Fetgatter, Gary Wells, and Graham Rouse.

Ken Fetgatter, who was probably the first to make fantasy balloon flowers on the Florist side of the isle (1986), has focused mainly on floral markets and is not generally known among balloonists.

Gary Wells, by virtue of (1) his early entry into Fantasy Flowers, (2) his crossover position as florist and balloonist, (3) the excellent quality of his work and (4) the promotion of Pioneer Balloon Company, has the name and style most often associated with the term "Fantasy Flowers" among balloonists today.

Graham Rouse, who was probably first with Fantasy Flowers (1983), comes from the balloonist side of the isle. He started in the balloon business with balloon flowers and continues to use and teach them (Look through the class notes from "How Does Your Garden Grow?" at IBAC 2002.) He has focused more energy on the abstract side of internal balloon structuring. That led to his one man art gallery exhibit in 1988, to a 1992 patent on specialized "Lite-Sculpture" technology and to current pending patents on newer balloon structuring technologies that will make their way into the industry
over the next few years. (You may view one of the earliest Fantasy Flowers and several of the Lite-Sculptures on the web at http://rouseinternational.com/rmsPhotos/index.html Look for "1983 Fantasy Flowers", "Sphere of Lites", "French Lites" and "Nite Lites".)
1983
-- Graham Rouse, then of ABC Creations in Raleigh, NC, makes his first internally wire structured balloon flowers. See "1983 Fantasy Flowers" on the lower part of the web page http://www.rouseinternational.com/rmsPhotos/index.html

1985
-- Graham Rouse publishes a series of greeting cards for balloon arrangements in which he coined the term "Fantasy Flowers" applied to balloon flowers.

1986
-- Graham Rouse is guest instructor for a series of classes in the Art Department of Meredith College in Raleigh, NC where he teaches internal structures in balloons to make abstract sculptures. This is followed by an artist's reception and photo exhibit of his balloon work and then a public exhibit of student work from the classes. -- Ken Fetgatter, AIFD, Bartlett, IL makes his first internally wire structured balloon flowers.

1987
-- Graham Rouse Fantasy Flower published in May issue of Balloons Today magazine
-- Graham Rouse internally structured abstract balloon design is the cover of the August issue of Balloons Today magazine
-- Graham Rouse teaches techniques at Unique Concepts Balloon Convention
-- Ken Fetgatter teaches internal wire structuring to make balloon flowers at an AIFD convention
-- Graham Rouse teaches internal structuring techniques at the West Coast Symposium of the National Association of Balloon Artists -- Graham Rouse teaches techniques at IBAC (known then as the Balloon and Singing Telegram Convention) and makes abstract versions as awards given by the convention to competition winners -- Probably it is in this year that Gary Wells and Ken Fetgatter first share ideas on internal structuring of balloons with each other.

1988
-- Graham Rouse exhibits abstract, internally structured balloon sculptures along with glass sculptures in local art gallery.
-- Graham Rouse has a three week, one man, public art gallery exhibit of balloon sculpture at the city art gallery in Rocky Mount, NC including internally structured balloon designs
-- Graham Rouse teaches internal structuring techniques at the National Association of Balloon Artists Convention

1989
-- Graham Rouse teaches internal structuring techniques at National Association of Balloon Artists Convention
-- Gary Wells and Ken Fetgatter do a joint presentation on Fantasy Flowers at AIFD convention

After these first seven years of Fantasy Flowers, internally structured balloon designs by many artists begin to show up in trade publications and balloon design competitions. The techniques and diversity of uses for internal structuring of balloons have multiplied greatly in the ensuing years.

Design

You may already be familiar with the design rules for florists and balloon artists, and it is important to carry some of these rules over when creating balloon flowers and figures. By following these simple rules your completed work will be more professional and pleasing to they eye.

Color:
Before making flowers and figures there is one very important element to consider in design work- and that is of course, color. Color can make or break your desired result. By using a color wheel, you will see which color combinations go well together and by following the "rules" will come up with a pleasing end result.

The use of primary colors are best used with children's parties, and secondary or tertiary colors with more sophisticated events. Don't forget black, grey, gold, and silver and white as well, and consider putting them in your designs if it is appropriate. Black and grey, as a rule, are more formal but can be depressing if too much of these colors are used.

Primary Colors: Red, Yellow, and Blue.

Secondary Colors: Violet, Orange, and Green.

Tertiary Colors: A mix of a primary and secondary color such as red-violet made with red and violet colors.

Shade: Hue mixed with black.

See the color wheel on the next page.

The 2/3, 1/3 rule:
This rule will help you make good decisions for the overall design, no matter what the size. The rule is to use 2/3 light colors and 1/3 dark colors in designs. By remembering to use this guideline, your finished décor won't seem overwhelming or heavy.

Balloon Flowers and Figures

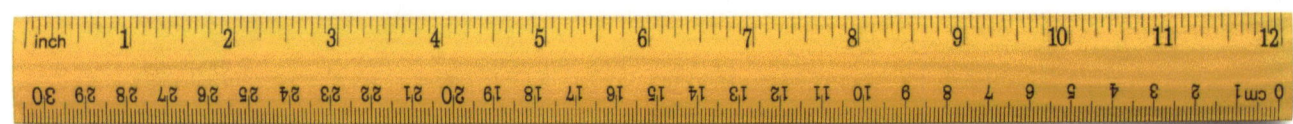

Kenishirotie—Fotolia.com

Scale and Proportion:
This rule covers the scale of the décor in relation to the location it is in, which includes the room, tables, stage, or other features to consider, or if the décor is outside. This may seem obvious, but use larger décor in big venues, and smaller décor in small venues. A huge floral balloon design in the center of a small table would be out of proportion and more suited to a buffet table or on the floor.

When doing small work such as figures for the top of a cake or a table centerpiece, keep proportion in mind as well, and make all of the elements fit together.

The 14" Rule:
For table centerpieces, be sure to follow the 14" rule and keep major design elements at or below this line so people can see each other across the table easily. Make sure any large items attached to the centerpiece and floating above the table are secured with a 50-lb test line or ribbon that does not block the view. Raise these elements high enough so that people sitting around the room can see the stage or podium, if applicable.

Having pointed out the "rules," don't be afraid to try something different when it is called for—a dramatic element that is unexpected can be a point of conversation.

Following is a color wheel, commonly used by professional designers.

Left:
While quite beautiful, this sample centerpiece arrangement does not follow the 14" rule, therefore, guests will have a difficult time conversing.

ruslan_iefremov-fotolia.com

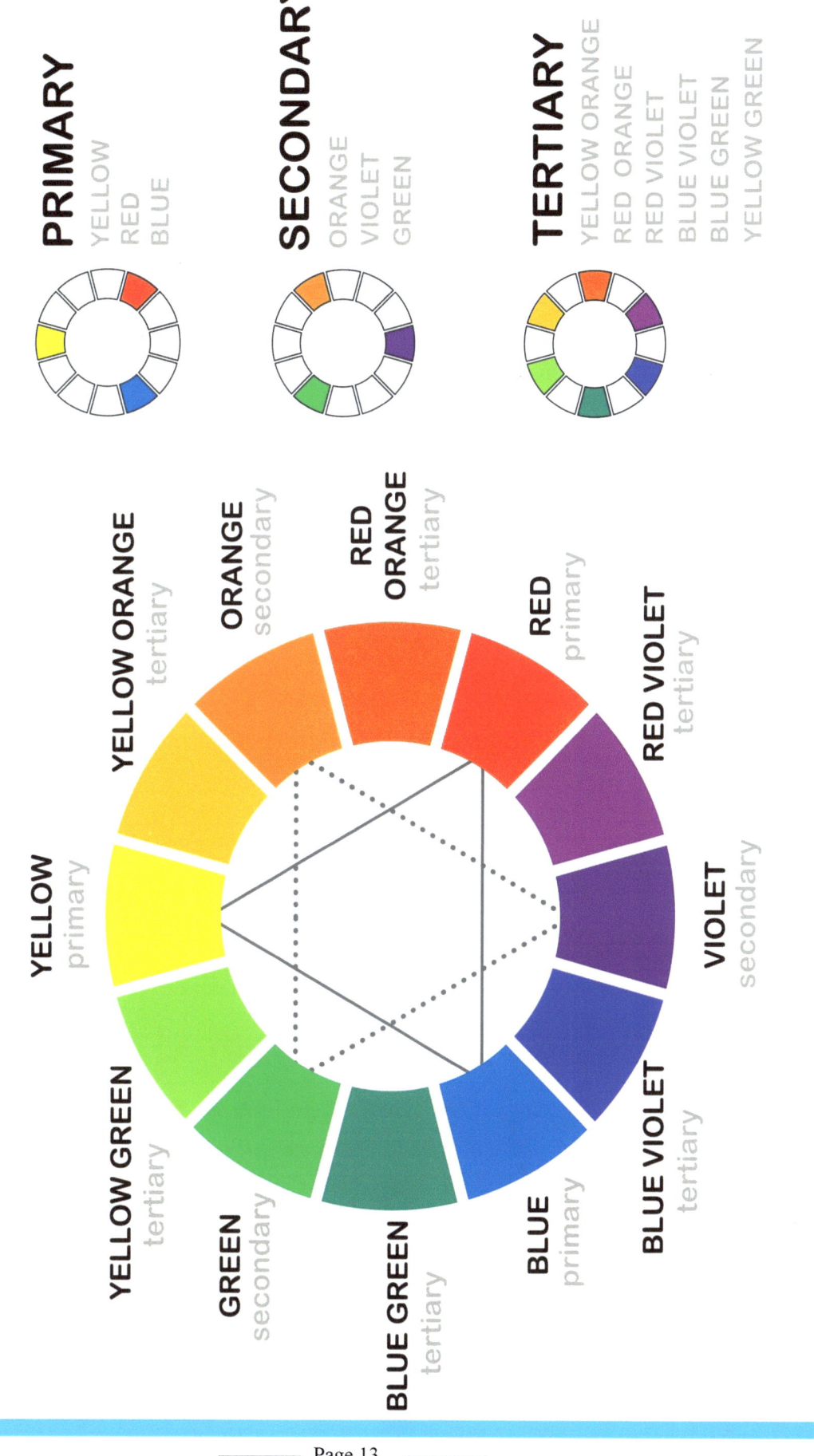

Tools and Supplies Needed to Construct Fantasy Flowers

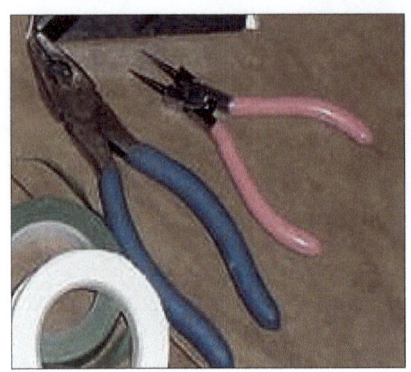

You may already have most, if not all of the supplies needed to make fantasy flowers, but check this list in case you need to purchase anything. You will easily find these items at hardware stores, wholesale and retail floral supply stores, and balloon shops.

Tools needed to make Fantasy Flowers:

- Large and small scissors (sharp)
- Small nail scissors (sharp)
- Tiny needle-nose pliers
- Small round-nose pliers
- Regular size needle-nose pliers
- Wire cutters
- Medium-temperature glue gun and glue sticks
- Hand balloon pump
- Nitrogen and/or helium tank with nozzle, or electric air inflator (if desired)
- Sizing template (if not using automatic sizer on elec. Inflator)

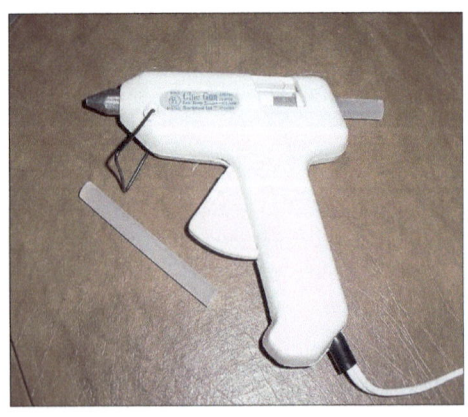

Balloon hand pumps are available in different styles from several balloon suppliers. Suppliers who specialize in twister/entertainer markets such as T. Meyers Magic will have the largest selection.

Supply and Tool List:

- 20, 18, and 16 gauge floral wire in 18" lengths
(Note, wire size gets SMALLER as the gauge gets larger)
18 gauge is used most often

- Green and white floral tape
- Binding wire (thin wire wrapped on a stick)
- Rubber cement
- Good quality 5", 11", and 16" round balloons in assorted colors
- Good quality 130, 260 and 350 balloons (animal or entertainer balloons) in assorted colors
- Nitrogen, air, or helium tanks as needed on stands or anchored to a wall
- Tank nozzles
- Professional nozzles and inflators if desired
- Sharp scissors
- Monofilament line (10lb and 50lb)
- Other supplies as desired
- Camera to take photos of your creations
- Hi-Float for helium-filled balloons

For finishing:

- Fabric ribbons
- Bridal tulle or gossamer
- Plastic or glass vases
- Green moss, Spanish moss, shred, and other items for covering mechanics in your designs
- Sharpie brand small tip markers for adding finishing touches

Hint: Sharpie brand pens are best for use on balloons because they do not break down latex. Available at most office supply stores.

How to Make Cluster Flowers

The cluster flower using inflated round balloons is super easy to make. Larger designs are a little more difficult, but with practice you'll get it down perfectly.

Use round balloons in sizes from 5" to 16". There are 18", 24", 3' and 40" balloons and larger, but these are too large to handle, and don't make a nice flower shape. I stick with the smaller sizes because they make a pear shape, rather than a perfectly round shape when inflated, and fit together better as petals.

Ingredients:

Five 16" red latex balloons
Two 11" yellow balloons
Ten yellow 260 balloons
Monfilament line
Three green 260 balloons
A weight

Recipe

Let's start with a flower made with 11" balloons. Gather five 11" latex balloons in red, and two 5" balloons in yellow or orange for the centers, high-float, heliim, monofilament line

1. Inflate the red balloons fully with air or nitrogen if hanging, or helium if floating, two at a time, and size them with a template or "eye-size." Eye-sizing is done without a sizer, and you compare the size of the balloons by holding one balloon next to the other and looking at the top and bottom of the balloon, letting air out until it is the same height as the first balloon.

This cluster was made with 16" overinflated balloons, sized to 15". An 11" balloon sized to 6" was used for the center on both sides, and we added stamens made with 260 balloons partially inflated.

Use Hi-Float inside the balloons (available at suppliers) to make this cluster last for several days The larger sizes are appropriate for large spaces such as stages or trade show halls.

Hi-Float is used by professional balloon artists. It is a substance that is inserted inside latex balloons to seal the interior so helium or air cannot escape.

Let some air out of each balloon. By inflating balloons fully until they are a pear shape, then letting some air out, the balloons will be more pliable and are less likely to pop. Now tie the two balloons together at the necks.

You can make any size cluster flower in this manner. Make a 4" balloon by deflating a 5" balloon to 4". For a 9" balloon, deflate an 11" balloon to 9", or use 16" balloons deflated to 14" for very large flowers.

2. Make a second pair of balloons in the same manner and the same size as the first pair.

3. Inflate a single balloon (your fifth to inflate) the same size, and tie it into one of the pairs, or "duplets," as we call them in the industry.

4. Twist the remaining duplet into the three balloons at the neck areas to make a cluster of five balloons. *A cluster of five balloons is more pleasing to the eye and more realistic than four balloons.*

5. Inflate the 5" yellow or orange balloons to 1 1/2" to 2" in diameter (or whatever size looks best to you) and tie these together in a duplet as close to the inflated portion of the balloon as possible. If you tie these together loosely they will not stay put. Now push this duplet into the center of the 5-balloon cluster, with one on each side of the cluster. The center balloons will hold the 5 balloons in place. Now you have a balloon flower that looks good from both sides.

Air-filled balloons can last for days.

Note: 5" and 7" balloons are too small for helium and won't float more than a few minutes, so don't use helium when using smaller balloons.

Margo Harrison– fotolia.com

The cluster flower above was made with five 11" balloons, with a second cluster of five 5" white balloons and one teal balloon tied to the center.

▶ **Tip:** If attaching a balloon cluster to a wall or anything that may pop the balloons, place clear packing tape on the back of the balloons before putting the design in place.

A Super Cluster Flower

For a large venue or outdoor event, super cluster flowers may be just the ticket.

To make this type of inflated flower, use air-filled balloons only. The number of smaller balloons used without helium will not allow this size flower to float. It will need to be suspended from above with monofilament line or attached to a column or structure.

Note: Small 5" balloons do not hold enough helium to float.

Alexander Yakovlev– Fotolia.com

To make:

1. Inflate seven 16" balloons with air or nitrogen, over-inflated and form into a cluster. You'll need the pear shape formed by over-inflating.
2. Make a second cluster of five to seven 11" balloons and attach it on top of the first cluster with monofilament line.
3. Make a third cluster of five 7" balloons and attach.
4. Blow up several more underinflated 5" balloons and tie them together at the necks, then pull into the cluster

Use pear-shaped balloons instead of round shaped balloons for this design

Flower Arches

Courtesy of Christopher Horne CBA - Professional Balloon Decorations", Northampton, England

This beautiful arch was made with giant flowers made with air and helium-inflated balloons - they are effectively topiary balls with either 260Q loops or sections of 350Q balloons inserted in the gaps.

Editors note: Note that some of the flowers are *Qualatex brand 11" Geo Blossom balloons* (top three balloons) which are available at most *Qualatex* Distributors. Make these by inflating the blossom, then adding two 5" balloons to the center. Inflate one 5" balloon, pull the neck through the center, then inflate the second balloon and tie it to the neck of the first. Now you have a blossom with a center that is quick and easy.

Christopher added 350 size balloons to the backs of the bigger flowers to make them seem even larger. Also notice the squiggly vines made with 260 green balloons at the top for added interest.

Use of Cluster Flowers in Design

If you want this type of flower to lay flat against something such as a wall, make one of the balloons in the center duplet (on the back) smaller than the one that will be showing in the front.

Attach the flower to balloon columns, metal, or fabric with double-sided tape. You may also tie a piece of curling ribbon or an un-inflated 260 animal balloon into the center of the cluster, and wrap the ribbon or 260 around other design elements to secure it.

Depending on the color and type of balloon used, you can use this flower in a lot of applications, from silly to sophisticated. Try using a few clusters in a balloon drop for a surprise effect.

Speed Tip: Make air-filled balloon flowers in advance of an event and store in plastic bags for up to a week until needed.

Giant Flower Clusters

- May be hung by monofilament line if filled with air.

- May be inflated with helium (11" or larger) instead of air. You may also use Hi-Float if you want to make several flowers in advance. The larger flowers take longer to make than the smaller 5", so allot extra time. When using helium, you will want to tie 50-lb monofilament (fishing line), and/or a ribbon or thin strip of tulle or cloth to the center section, then pull down through two of the balloons in the large cluster. Glue the cloth with cool glue or a *Glue Dot* (available from balloon suppliers). You may need to put a dab of glue or double-sided clear tape between each cluster balloon to help keep them in place. You will need to tie this cluster down to a weight. The simplest weight to make is sand or rocks placed inside a double-baggy and then covered with mylar or fabric material. You may also used a water-filled double-stuffed 16" balloon or two for a weight as well.

Cluster Flower Features

1. Add one or more wide **green ribbons** to simulate a stem.

2. Add balloon leaves made out of 260 animal balloons. Use one inflated 260, tie the two ends together, twist to make two loops, and attach to the ribbon.

3. Add a vine stem made out of 260 balloons by inflating, then letting a little air out, tie, and wrap tightly around your arm to make a squiggle. Alternatively, wrap the Un-inflated balloon around your finger, wrist or cardboard gift wrap tube and inflate. This is easier to do with two people. Tie ends together of the 260 balloons to make longer vines.

4. Add stamens by making a cluster of 5 partially inflated 260 balloons and inserting them into the open gaps behind the flower center.

5. Add stamens by inflating a 1 1/2" bubble of 260 or 350 balloons, tie and place a cluster of these in the center.

6. Add a tulle bow or ribbons for wedding designs. You can drape thin lengths of tulle between flowers if desired.

7. Add loops of inflated 260 balloons around or through the finished flowers.

8. Add 350 balloons to the backs of large flowers.

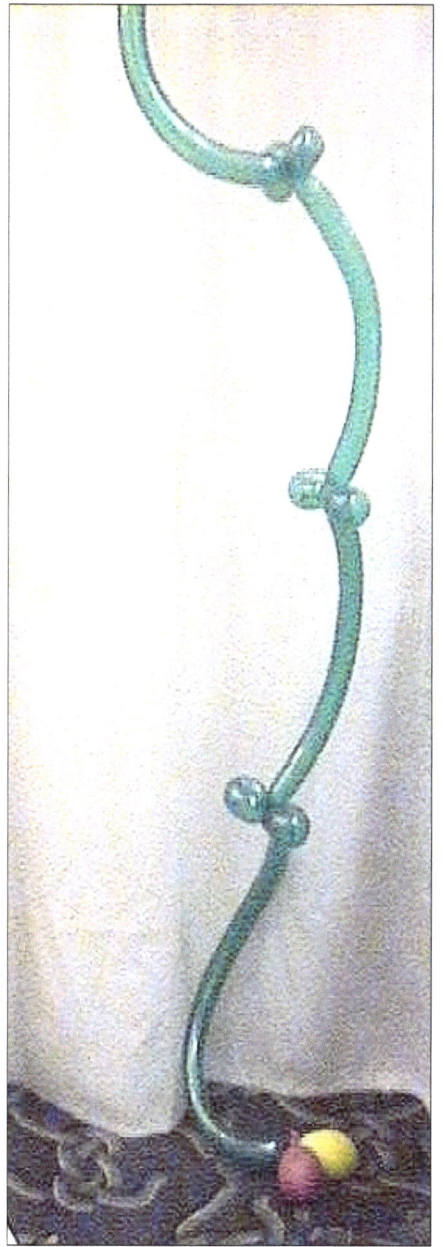

This vine stem was attached to a large helium-filled cluster with 16" round balloons. A 50-lb. Monofilament line is attached to the flower and then to water-filled balloon weights at the bottom. The 260 balloon vine was attached to the base of the flower then to the weight. The fishing line is not noticeable when the design is complete.

Balloon Flowers and Figures

Stage Backdrop Designs with Flowers

Make a background for a stage by varying the lengths of the ribbon or monofilament line that giant 11" or 16" balloon flowers are attached to.

Use sets of three, five, or seven (or any odd –number combination) for a visually appealing design. Vary the heights of the flowers, with the tallest in the center.

Set up stage flowers based on the event and mood desired.

Sample stage designs:

A set of five flowers all the same height in a single row is unnatural and rigid-looking. I wouldn't suggest it for most décor.

A set of five flowers in a graduating size pattern is attractive, and it draws the eye to the center of the stage.

A set of seven flowers in a alternating heights is also attractive, yet has a more uniform look to it.

Balloon Flowers and Figures

Make a forest of flowers for a large stage production!
The stage can set the mood for the entire show.

Note: Stage sets are one of my favorite things to do. Imagine a scene with the actors playing tiny fairies, elves, or leprechauns—even Thumbelina or Peter Pan—your giant balloon flowers and trees will create the perfect backdrop!

Use four 24" latex balloons for a really BIG flower!

Twisted Flowers

This method has been used by twisters and entertainers for many years, but decorators can learn to make them, too. The balloons used are usually 260 size (2" wide x 60" long when fully inflated) balloons, but you may also use 160's (1" wide x 30" long) or 350's (3" wide x 50" long). These are also known as "animal" or "entertainer" balloons, and can be found at most balloon party shops or online. If you plan to do a lot of work with these I highly suggest using the best quality product you can find (see a list of suppliers in the back of this book).

Ingredients
- Animal balloons in the colors and size(s) of your choice
- Green balloons for stems
- An air-inflator for balloons
- Plastic bags to keep the flowers fresh after they are made

Balloon air-inflators are inexpensive and can usually be found at party stores. It is hard to inflate the smaller 130 balloons without a smaller size inflator, though. You can get any size inflator from BalloonBuoy.com, or other internet sites and balloon wholesalers.

If you are a professional balloon artist, consider getting a rubber-tip nozzle for 260's (the size you will use most often) and use it on a nitrogen tank. You may also use a professional electric air inflator that can be purchased from wholesale suppliers.

The Easy 8-petal flower

Instructions

1. Inflate a 260 balloon to 1" from the end, and hold onto the neck. Let some air out to make a soft bubble (this makes the balloons easier to work with and less likely to pop). Twist a bubble 1" from the neck end and hold at the twist, then let the air out of the very end.

This makes a longer neck to tie with and it is much easier to handle. Now tie the balloon together with the 1" tip and the neck end.

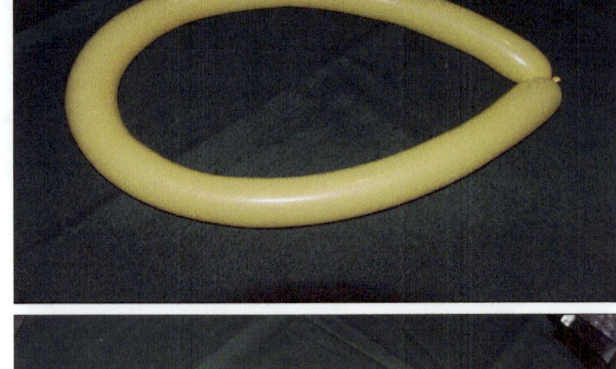

2. Hold the tied portion with one hand, find the opposite side with the other hand and twist the balloon a little at this point.

3. Bring both centers together and twist two to three times.

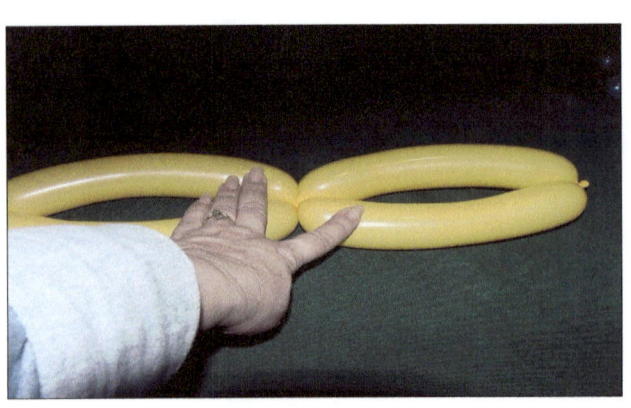

4. Grab the balloon on the opposite side of the twist and push towards the twist, then twist all of these portions together. If the balloon pops or is too tight to work with, just get another balloon and start over.

Don't worry, with a little practice you will get the correct size down quickly.

5. To make an 8-petal flower, just make another 4-petal flower in the same or contrasting color, then push one flower into the other. This takes a little practice. I use a table and push one down on top of the other. You may need to turn the flower over to complete the process.

You will need to pull two petals apart from the bottom flower while pushing a petal from the top flower between them.

Stem:
Inflate a 260 balloon to 12" and twist a 1" bubble at the end. Push the bubble to the center of the flower and pull the twisted section through to the center. The remainder of the 260 is the stem.

The Easy 6-Petal Flower

1

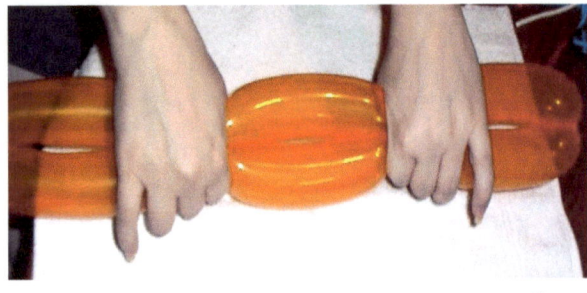
2

3

Instructions:

1. Inflate a 260 balloon to 1" from the end, and hold onto the neck. Let more air out than the 4-petal flower to make a very soft bubble. Twist a bubble 1" from the neck end and hold at the twist, then let the air out of the very end. This makes a longer neck to tie with and it is much easier to handle. Now tie the balloon together with the 1" tip and the neck end.

2. Hold the tied portion with one hand, find the opposite side with the other hand and twist the balloon a little at this point.

3. Now dividing the balloon in thirds, twist three equal portions of the two long bubbles together.

4. Place each of the three portions on top of each other in a folded manner as in the photo at the right.

4

5. Holding one twisted portion with one hand, push the opposite side in with the other hand and twist all of these sections together. This makes a 6-petal flower and you don't need to add another flower section as with the 4-petal flower.

Right: finished flower portion

Finish the flower with center and/or stem as in the following instructions.

Add a Center, Stem, and Leaves

How to make a flower center, stem, and leaves using one single balloon — a real time saver!

1. Inflate a green 260 (or whatever size you are working with), let a little air out of the balloon, and tie. Twist either the tied end or the top end in a 1 1/2" to a 2" bubble, depending on the size flower center you want. Twist several times.

2. Push this twisted bubble at the twist between two of the flower petals until the balloon is centered. Leave the stem towards the back if you want the petal to face up, or push between two stems to make the flower face forward.

Balloon Flowers and Figures

3. Leaves: Find a good place for two leaves, and make a twist with several turns. Now make a 2" or so bubble and twist again.

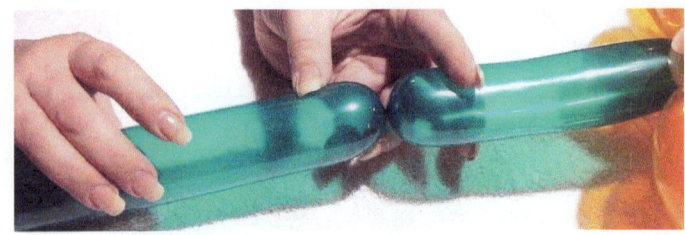

4. Bring the two twisted parts of the balloon together, and twist them together two or three times. This makes your first leaf. If you want the stem to stand up straight, make a second leaf the same way on the opposite side of the first leaf, twisting it into the same area.

If you want the stem to bend and twist, just make a second leaf further down on the stem.

Above: Pushing the stem into the flower from the side.

Finished!

Page 30

Flower Stems and Stamens

How to add a stem

To a balloon that already has a center: Blow up a green balloon fully, let a little bit of air out of the balloon, then twist a 2" or 3" bubble at the end and tie close to the inflated portion. Now use this 2" or 3" end to wrap into the center of the flower. Just wrap it around several times—there is no need to tie it in. Pull the stem down between two flower petals if desired.

Make flower center

Push your finger into the knot end of the balloon, and grab the knot with your other hand through the balloon about 2" from the end. Now twist the knot into the balloon. Push into the flower center as above. *Note: it is easier if you wet your finger prior to pushing it inside the balloon.*

To add leaves

Just twist a 3" - 4" bubble in the green stem balloon about 1/3 of the way down from the top of the flower. Twist a couple of times at the top, then twist again 3-4" down, and bring these two twisted sections together and twist again a couple of times. This makes one leaf. Make a second leaf directly opposite this one if you want the stem to stand up straight, or a little further down if you want it to bend.

Photo: Sinisa Botas –Fotolia.com

Make a round center

Method 1: (double sided) Inflate two 5" round balloons to the size of 1 1/2" and tie together tightly. Push this duplet into the center of the flower. Hang the flower with monofilament line or ribbon

Method 2: (single sided) Inflate one 5" round balloon to the size of 1 1/2" and tie into the center of the flower cluster. Use this to attach to walls or balloon columns with double-sided tape, or as a corsage.

Balloon Flowers and Figures

Make a Stamen Center

Method 1: (shown at left) Blow a puff of air into a 260 balloon and tie. Blow up a very small round balloon and tie to the end of the 260 balloon. Cut of the neck ends. Use different colors for a striking effect. Use these for the centers of flowers, or use to fill in space between flowers in an arrangement.

Method 2: Blow a puff of air into three or more 260 balloons and tie. Push these in between two of the flower petals. Use full-length balloons for double-sided flowers, or cut off half of the balloons for single-sided flowers.

Method 3: (shown at right) Inflate a 1" bubble in a 260 balloon and tie. Repeat so you have a total of three stamens. Push this cluster in between two of the flower petals.

For the flower above I simply used uninflated left over 260 balloons that had been cut for other uses.

Flower Arrangements

(right) Make a floral arrangement using different flower styles. This container has a 130 6-petal flower with 260 stamens and an added 130 stem with leaves (bottom), a 6-petal 260 flower with combination flower center and stem with a green 260, and an 8-petal 260 flower with combination center, stem and leaves.

I like to add green "leaves" or stems for filler by inflating 260 balloons to within a few inches of the top. These act as filler and make your designs more interesting. This is a plastic vase. If you need more weight to hold plastic vases down, add rocks or heavy metal washers to the bottom.

(left) a 350 six-petal flower with a couple of extra green stems makes a nice big arrangement for large areas such as a stage or near a podium. This would also work well on a buffet table. These balloons are so tall, that they can easily be used in floor designs and walkways for malls, Easter or garden events.

Floral Bouquets

Fotolia.com

For this cute design, make a five-cluster air-filled base with a hidden weight attached to the center. Make a bunch of cluster flowers on stems, place the stems into the base, and wrap with 260Q balloons tied at the back to hold them in place. Add a string of tiny bubbles formed with a 360 balloon. Note the grapes formed with 260 balloons. Make one or two flowers out of a cluster of four balloons with wire inside to hold their shape.

Margie Padgitt

Pastel colors in this group are appropriate for a ladies tea or garden party

This A-symmetrical design is made with four cluster flowers made with 5" latex balloons, big looped flowers made with 260 balloons and centers made with deflated 5" balloons. It would be appropriate to frame an entranceway or lead people to a door.

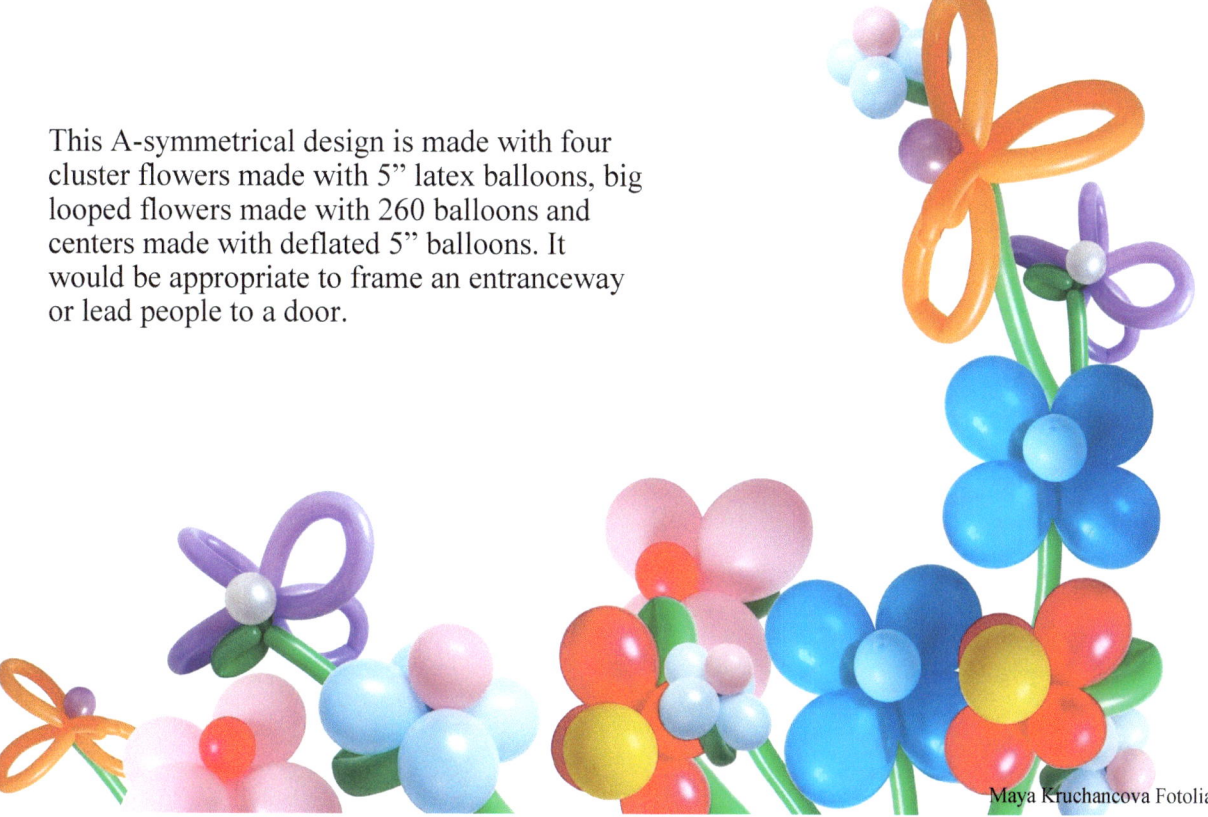

Maya Kruchancova Fotolia

Balloon Flowers and Figures

Design ideas–
Place duplicate designs on either side of a doorway for a welcoming entrance:

A bouquet of brightly colored flowers is appropriate when you want to make a big statement. These are great to give as a long-lasting gift. Air-inflated balloon flowers can last for weeks.

Yurakp—Fotolia.com

Use of one color (in this case purple) combined with other colors in each flower draws the eye to the design.

Extras to go with Balloon Flowers

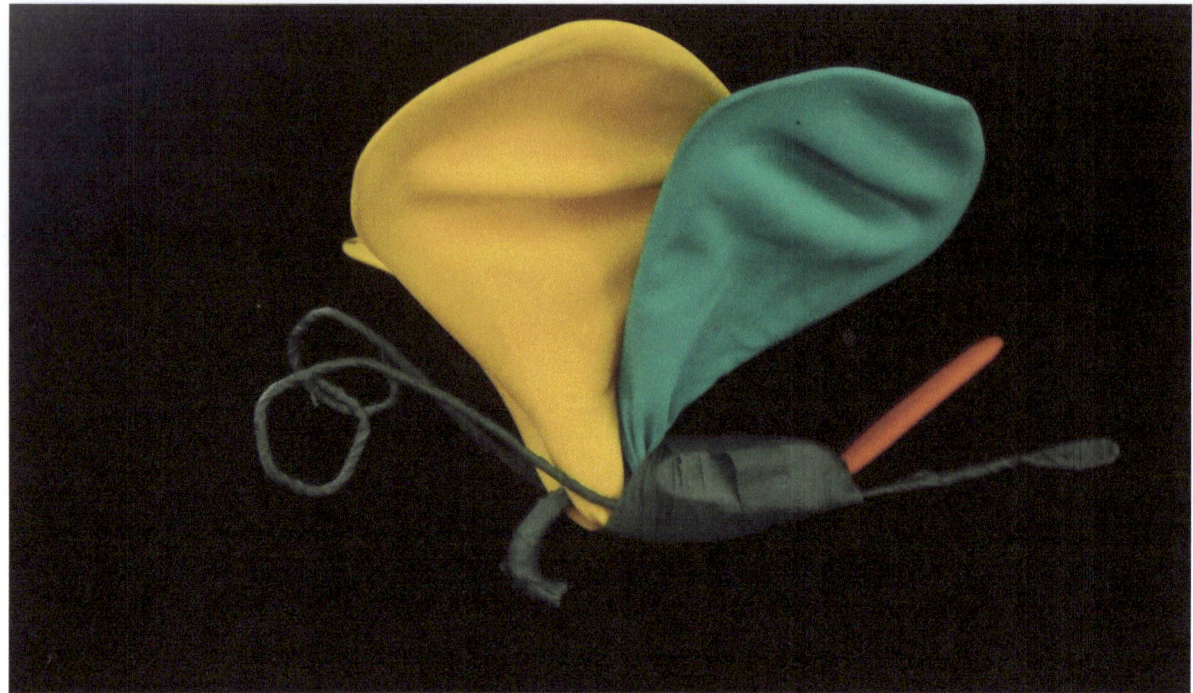

This butterfly was created with 11" balloons, 18 gauge wire, and green floral tape using the same techniques for flower construction. Note that one back leg has not been covered with a balloon in order to show the construction. For the antenna and proboscis, cover wire with floral tape and bend into shape. (See the section on wired flowers for more information)

Left: A snail constructed entirely of inflated 260 balloons twisted together. Use three or four different colors to add interest—after all these are *fantasy* creatures.

Margie Padgitt

Left: This cute bee was made with inflated 5" balloons for the head and body, an inflated 260 balloon for the wings, and two uninflated 260 balloons with the neck ends left on for antenna. Squiggly eyes are glued on and a face and body stripes were made with a black sharpie pen.

Right: Giant bugs made with inflated 350 balloons stacked on top of poles on bases. The eyes were made with inflated 11" round balloons. The antenna were made with partially inflated 350 balloons.

These could be made on a much smaller scale using 260 balloons for the body and antenna, and 5" round balloons for the eyes.

Use you imagination to create not only flowers, but things that go along with them for added interest that guests won't forget.

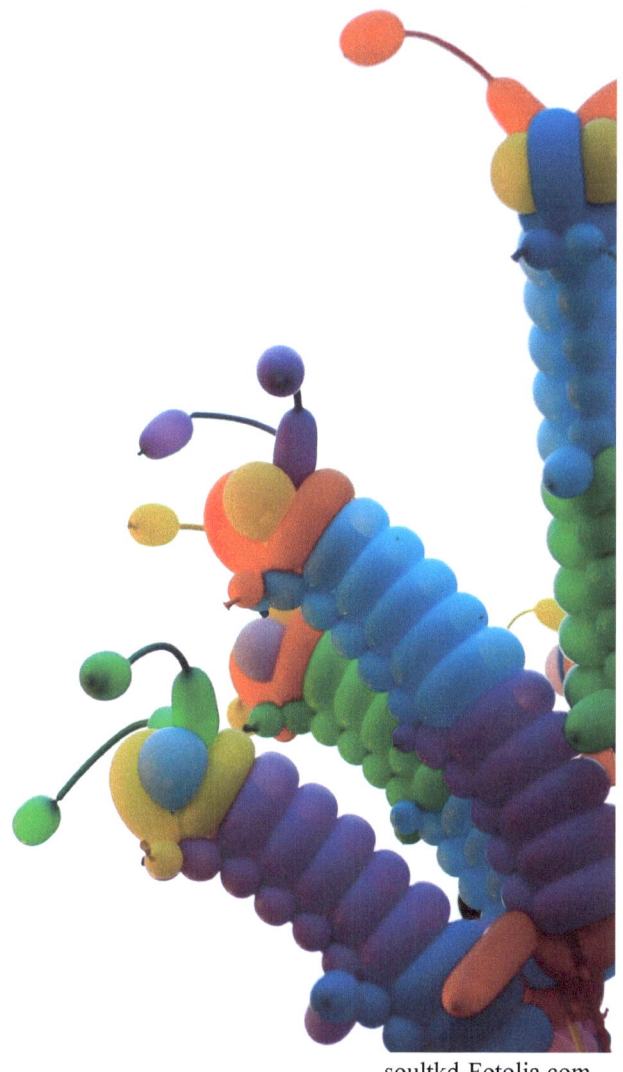

soultkd-Fotolia.com

A Distortion Technique

Here's something really impressive that you can use for your higher-priced décor jobs. This distortion technique was developed by Graham Rouse in 1983.

The method used to create the "leaves" at in the photo at the right uses a stabilizing wire inside a 260 balloon. The unique shape is created by inflating the balloon partially with air, then pulling and stretching it over the wire.

Experiment with this method to get the results you are looking for.

The shaping of the 260 balloon bases in the photo above is possible because the balloon is partially inflated as well as being stretched over the internal structure. By using this technique, a base is created to hold up the flowers.

Margie Padgitt

Courtesy of Graham Rouse, Rouse International, Columbia, SC, USA

This arrangement has internally structured stems to provide longer lasting and thinner support for the flowers. Notice the exchanges of color between pink and purple.

Balloon Flowers and Figures

Courtesy Graham Rouse, Rouse International, Columbia, SC,

This is a black flower arrangement that Graham designed for a customer who wanted to kid a friend about getting older, yet wanted something more sophisticated than dead flowers. The stems for all the balloon flowers and foliage are structured internally to provide longer lasting support than would be normal for inflated balloons without reinforcement. Also the narrow internal structures made it possible to grow the arrangement out of a small, plastic champagne glass.

Water and Wire

Graham put some water in an apple balloon, added some air and then did an apple twist. This balloon forms the base. He then used a section of balloon straw inside a stretched and partially inflated #260 to make the stem.

The stem is inserted into the core of the apple base and pinched between petals of a #160 flower at the top to complete the arrangement. It is simple, economical, attractive, fairly stable and completely mobile.

Graham says that "Both air and water are fluids. They can both be easily shaped by containers. Air is, however, much lighter and much more easily compressed. I most often use water for the weight. I put water in balloons that are being used as a base for an arrangement. This can make the arrangement more stable and less likely to get knocked over, You could accomplish similar results with sand."

Water can also be used to create interesting lighting and color effects within balloons. A couple of times we even used larger balloons with water and goldfish inside. Presumably, water filled balloons will last longer than air filled balloons, because it is harder for the water to escape the balloons than for air to escape the balloons due to the size of the water or air molecules.

Visit the Rouse International website at www.rouseinternational.com for more information on Graham's latest products for balloon artists.

Balloon Flowers and Figures

More Ideas

Make a cute **starfish** by tying five individual 260 balloons together at the center. Add two white bubbles for the eyes and one small blue bubble for the mouth and draw a face on with a sharpie pen.

(Below) Small 5" cluster flowers tied into a wall of balloons add interest and detail to large décor.

Make a **simple flower** by inflating four 260 balloons and tying their ends together, then attach a stem in the center.

Create a whimsical caterpillar with 130 balloons inflated and twisted together with tiny bubbles between them. Add eyes with partially inflated 130 balloons. Place on a bendable wire.

A Ladybug

This cute ladybug can be used anywhere in a floral design, including on a flower.

Ingredients:
Black 260 balloon
White 260 balloon
Red 260 balloon
Two peach 260 balloons
Black sharpie pen
One 260 balloon to match the color of the flower

Hint: to make a smaller ladybug use 130 balloons instead of 260 balloons.

Instructions:
1. Inflate a black 260 balloon to 1/3 the length and tie off. Make a small 1" bubble for the neck and two 2" bubbles for the body and twist together, make two more 2" bubbles and twist for the back of the body.
2. Inflate a red 260 balloon to 1/4 the length and tie on to the back of the black bubbles. Make two 2" bubbles and twist, then attach to the top of the black body.
3. Add a two bubble white balloon for the eyes.
4. Add two peach balloons inflated only 1" and tie into the body for the antenna.
5. Make a face and dots with the black marker.
6. Tie the ladybug on to the flower with the matching color 260 if desired.
7. Trim off excess balloon ends.

Design Applications

130 Balloon Flowers:

- Make tiny 6-petal flowers using 130 balloons to use as corsages.
- Use 130 balloon flowers for centerpiece work since the larger 260 balloons are often too large to use in centerpieces.
- Use balloon flowers for pew decorations, with a tulle bow behind each one.
- Attach lots of 130-balloon flowers to the side of balloon columns in your décor work to add more detail to your work.

Hint: 130 balloons do not stay looking good very long so make them the day of or the day before the event. The air escapes these balloons fairly quickly.

260-Balloon Flowers:

- Make a plastic or glass vase full of twisted flowers on stems for a buffet or table arrangement.
- Attach a few 260-balloon flowers to the side of balloon columns in your décor work to add more detail to your work.
- Attach a 260 flower to the bottom of 10-lb. monofilament or long balloon ribbon attached to a 16" helium balloon. Use lots of these floating on a ceiling over a dance floor for a fun look. You may want to use mostly ribbons alone, and just a few with flowers. Experiment to see what looks best to you.

Hint: 260 balloons stay looking good for a few days if kept inside a plastic sack. You can make many flowers up ahead of time to save time the day of the job or event.

350-Balloon Flowers:

- Use these fat, larger flowers for a funky 70's theme party.
- Use where you need larger visual effects, such as a stage area. Make vases out of covered popcorn tins, fill with 350 flowers on stems, and place on a stage, or in outdoor décor areas where bigger is better.

Hint: These balloons are a little harder to handle than 260's, so allow extra time to make flowers. You may also make these up ahead of time and keep them in plastic bags.

How to Make
Wired Fantasy Balloon Flowers

Wired Balloon Flowers

Fantasy wire balloon flowers are made with un-inflated latex balloons with a bent wire inside. Use 18 or 16 gauge wire only, as thinner gauges will not hold their shape. The larger the gauge, the thinner the wire. The technique takes a little practice, but after you have made a few you will get the hang of it and your speed will increase. This type of balloon flower takes longer to make than others, but the results are well worth it. And when you hear your client or guests exclaim "That's made out of *balloons*?!" you'll know that you have a winner.

Wired flowers can be made up several weeks in advance of an event as long as they are kept sealed in a plastic bag to keep them from oxidizing and breaking down. If cloth-wrapped floral wire is used, it won't show through as much as plain wire does. Alternatively, you may wrap the wire with a thin covering of floral tape. If the flowers are to be used right away use unwrapped wire.

Remember to keep bulk down when creating the petals, so when you put them together the finished product looks elegant rather than bulky. Do this by cutting off the entire neck of the balloon and pull the balloon very tightly over the wire so it has a smooth finished appearance.

The finished flower size depends on the size of balloon you start with. Unlike inflated balloons that can be sized down to the desired size, there is little play with size when making wired balloon flowers. A 5" balloon makes a small flower, an 11" balloon makes a medium size flower, and a 16" bal-

loon makes a large flower.

Supplies Needed:
5", 11", and 16" latex balloons in any color or style.
260 and 350 size latex balloons in white, green, yellow, and orange
18 and 16 gauge floral wire (available from floral supply stores in 18" lengths)
Cloth-wrapped 18 and 16 gauge floral wire if available
Wire cutters
Needle-nose pliers
Sharp Scissors
Floral tape in white and green
Thin floral binding wire

Wired Fantasy Flower Technique

Recipe for A Rosebud
(or beginning portion of most flowers)

-4 11" balloons in your choice of color
-5 18" pieces of 18 ga. Floral wire
- Thin floral binding wire (on a stick)
-Floral tape
-Needle nose pliers
-Scissors

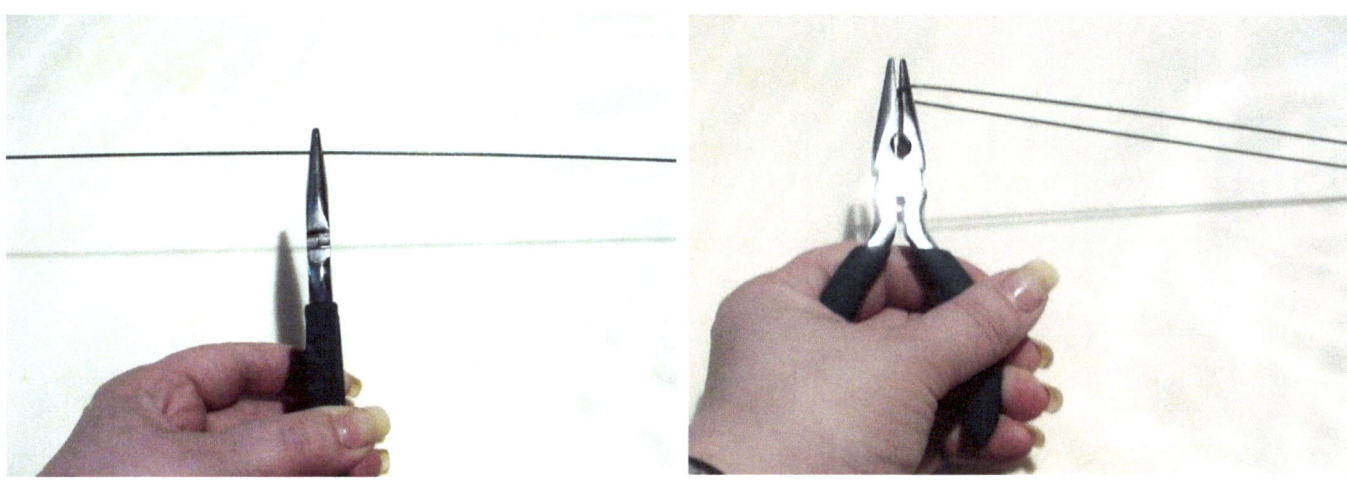

Step 1. Bend a length of 18" 18– gauge floral wire in half using needle-nose pliers, dowel rod or other object, based on if you want the finished petal to have a small pointed end or larger rounded end. Bend all petal wires using the same tool for a uniform look. Once floral wire has been bent it is impossible to straighten it again so if you mess up a piece discard it and start over.

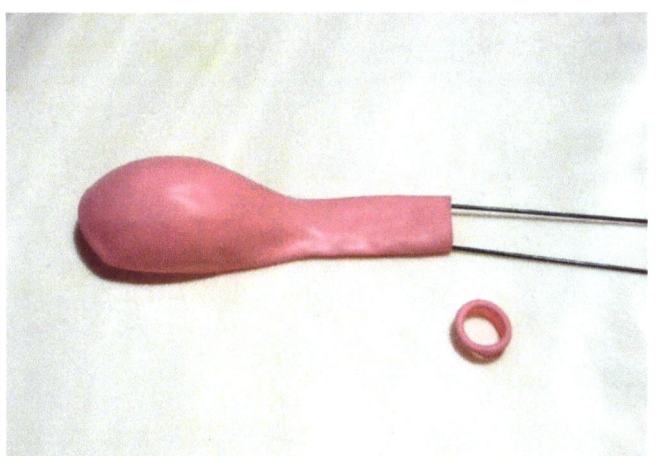

Step 2. Cut the lip end off of a latex balloon (this photo shows an 11" balloon) and insert the wire into the petal closed end first.

Note: If you cut the ENTRE neck end off the balloon (not shown) the result will be a tighter and smoother petal.

Step 3. Grip the rounded end with your thumb and forefinger and **s**tretch and pull the balloon over the wire very tightly. Wrap the end with binding wire (thin wire available at wholesalers and hobby stores). Floral tape will not hold larger petals, however tape will hold 260's and 5" latex balloons, so you may use it on the smaller balloons to hold them in place instead.

Note: I find it easier to grab the balloon and wire 1" from the end with one hand, while pulling from the neck with the other hand.

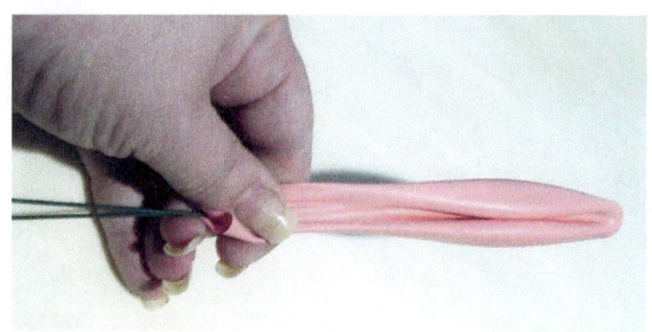

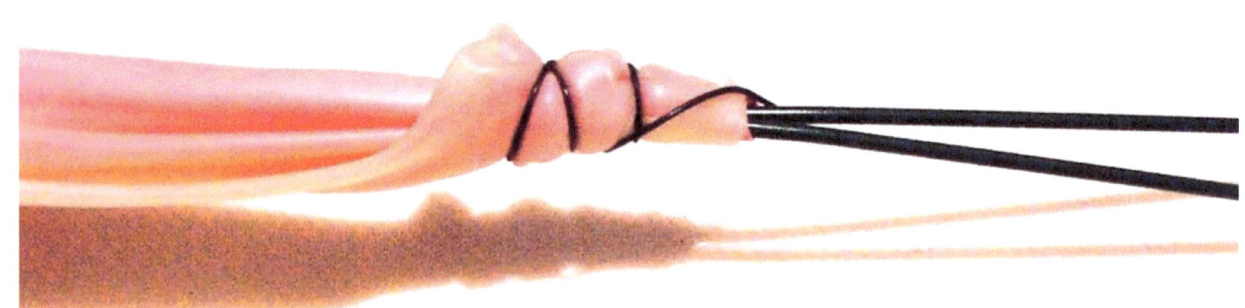

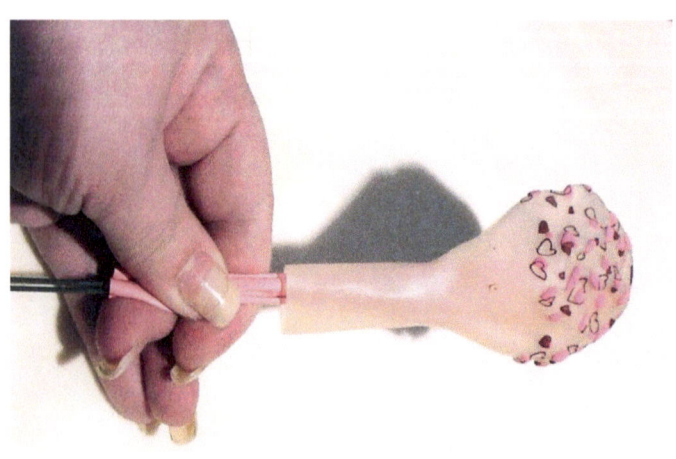

Step 4. If desired, place a clear balloon with a design on it over the solid color balloon petal you just made. Below are samples of three petals—one is just the clear balloon, one has a pink balloon inside a clear, and one has a red balloon inside a clear balloon. The clear balloon has red and white hearts on it. I used this for Valentine's Day.

Pull the wires apart through the balloons to make a petal shape, then bend back. Wrap with binding wire and tape.

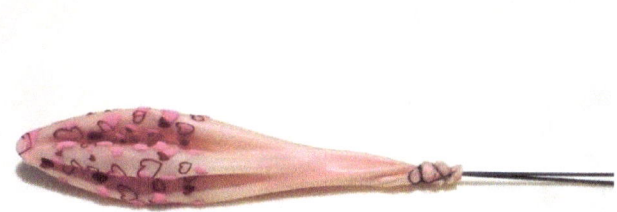

Step 5. For the flower center, simply pull balloons over the wire and do not pull the wires apart. This is just one style of flower center, but it works well for a rose. Bind the base with binding wire.

Step 6. Grasp the two wires inside the balloon and pull the wire apart, forming a petal shape.

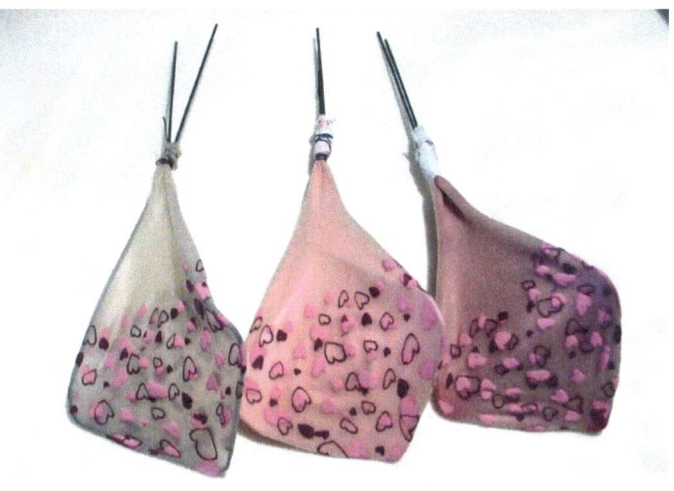

Step 7. Attach one petal to the flower center with floral tape. Remember to stretch and pull the floral tape to make it stick. It doesn't matter which side of the tape you use. Add one petal at a time, overlapping petals.

The finished product is a three-petal flower. Since it has a lot of detail with the printed balloons, I would not add any more petals. The addition of leaves would be sufficient. For a bouquet or arrangement, mix this type of flower with plain-petal flowers for a dramatic effect.

Wired Fantasy Flower Samples

(Right) Courtesy Cheryl A. Rupple, CBA
C3 Decorating in Defiance, Ohio

This **tropical design** with yellow wired fantasy flowers is a nice conversation piece. It is fun to watch guests when they discover that décor items are not what they may seem at first.

Below: **Fantasy five-petal Lily** made with squared-off wire at the tips of the petals. The stamens are yellow 260 balloons with a puff of air inside.

Attach the stamens to the first petal before adding the remaining petals. Add two leaves and wrap all with floral tape to finish off the look.

This type of flower is excellent for putting into floral foam or Styrofoam.

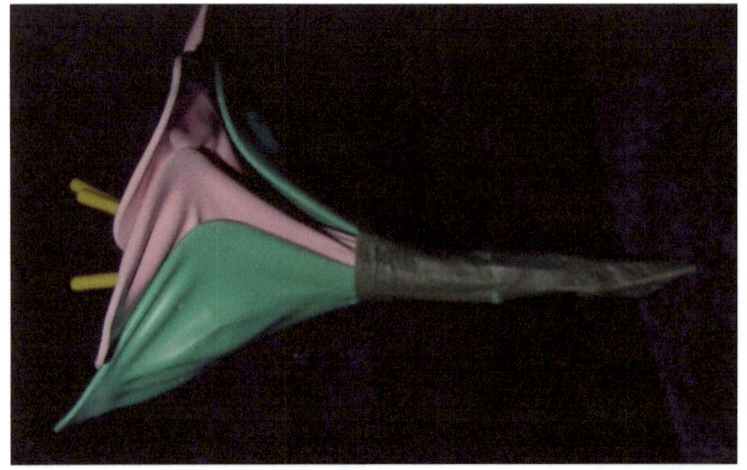

Margie Padgitt

Orchid Corsage: This was created as a birthday present for a good friend of Cris' to wear at her birthday party. It is a representation of a cymbidium orchid made from 5" balloons stretched over 16 gauge floral wire.

Courtesy Christopher Horne CBA - Professional Balloon Decorations, Northampton, England

Iris: This beautiful flower was created to show the technique of using an un-inflated 260Q balloon stretched over the finished petal to create a textured stripe.

Courtesy Christopher Horne CBA - Professional Balloon Decorations, Northampton, England

Wired clusters: I used one large 7-petal flower for the center, and 3-petal flowers around it in both designs. All petals were made with 11" latex balloons and 16 gauge wire.

Splashes of single-color flowers can make a dramatic statement.

Balloon Flowers and Figures

Inspiration From Nature

Look at samples from nature to get ideas for your fantasy flowers. You can try to match them exactly, but don't worry too much about it — fantasy flowers are just that—*Fantasy* creations.

Margie Padgitt

Wedding Flowers

The wired balloon flower method is especially suited to weddings because these flowers are more realistic looking, and are a good size to use in bouquets, boutonnières, pew flowers, corsages, centerpieces and altar arrangements.

Since they can be made ahead of time, you can add this service to your bridal orders without taking away from time needed on the job. Be sure to keep them in plastic to protect them from the air, which oxidizes latex balloons. These balloons keep for months if stored in plastic. You might even deliver them to the bride the night before or a few days before the wedding!

Bridal Bouquet Recipe

Ingredients:
45 5" white pearl latex balloons
5 white 260 balloons
18 gauge floral wire
Silk ivy
Bouquet holder with Styrofoam center

1. Make flower petals using 18" wire inside of the 5" latex balloons as described in the method.

2. Bend one petal inward from the sides and bend the top down slightly to form the center petal. Make five of these petals.

3. gather the center petal and three surrounding petals together and wire tightly.

4. Add the additional petals, one at at time, and wire together.

5. Wrap the stem with green floral tape.

6. Make five loops by placing a wire inside a 260 balloon, bending it around so the ends meet, and wire together.

7. Insert the flowers, loops, and purchased ivy into the bouquet holder.
Use this technique for many different styles of flowers. Add tulle, ribbons, or other types of greenery for different looks.

A Wedding Cake Topper

Balloon flowers, leaves and squiggles make a beautiful cake topper. Johnna Perry made individual roses and leaves, then assembled them for the top of this cake, which is wonderful keepsake for the bride.

Johnna made similar flowers for the rest of the wedding décor.

Note: The bride wanted this done in a certain way—it would have been Johnna's preference to make the squiggles smaller.

Photos and design Courtesy of Johnna Perry, Up Up and Away Balloons in Liberty, Missouri

Note: Balloon flower cake toppers may be used for birthday cakes, too!

A beautiful rose—this is a close-up of one of the roses on the wedding cake top. It is made with 5" latex wired balloons using the same techniques described earlier. The rosebud center is made with two balloons, rolled and folded without wire inside.

Wedding Card Bird Cage Flowers

Recipe for Birdcage:

1. Make roses in three sizes for this piece: the smallest is made from two 5" balloons; for the middle size an 11" balloon; for the largest, add 16" balloons in addition to the 11" balloons. These are all un-inflated latex balloons.

2. Slip a 5" balloon over a piece of bent 20 gauge floral wire, pull taut, and tape to the wire.

3. Cut a tiny hole in the top of a second 5" balloon and slip the first balloon, wire end first, through the hole. When the 2 balloons meet, the outside balloon folds into itself, making them look like a rosebud. Each balloon after the first is added the same way, and is attached with floral tape to the wire in the first balloon.

4. Silk rose leaves are taped on last, and everything is wired to the birdcage along with tulle and silk or wired leaves, and a purchased dove.

Photo and design by Maggie Brusa, CBA
The Balloon Platoon, Worcester, MA

Margie Padgitt

Calla Lilly
Great for weddings!

Ingredients:
One 16" pearl white balloon
One 260 or 350 size pastel yellow balloon
One piece 16 ga. floral wire
One piece 18 ga. floral wire
White and green floral tape
Binding wire

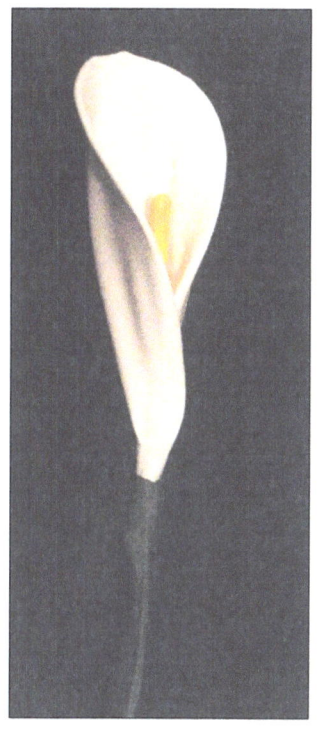

Recipe:

1. Bend the 16 ga. Wire in half around a drinking glass so you get a wide round shape. Form the tip into a peak.

2. Pull the 16" white pearl balloon over the wire and stretch and pull, then wrap binding wire around the neck to hold it.

3. Bend an 18 ga. Floral wire in half and place 1/2 of a 260 yellow pastel balloon over it.

4. Bind with wire or tape, but do not stretch too tightly. Place this stamen inside the white petal and bend the petal sides around it.

5. If you want the front to be more open, first tape with white floral tape for approximately 1/2", then add green floral tape.

Make the "stem" longer if desired by adding 18 or 16 gauge wire and cover completely with green floral tape.

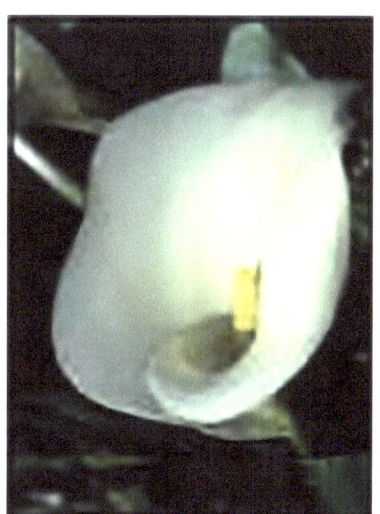

HINT: *Use photos of real flowers to get ideas for making fantasy balloon flowers. I get mine from www.clipart.com*

A Lovely Wedding Bouquet

Laura Caldwell (AKA Annie Banannie) of ACME Balloon Company in Southern California made this beautiful bouquet of fantasy flowers for her Las Vegas wedding in 2006 with the assistance of fellow balloon artist Patty Sorell.

The flowers each have five white petals and three yellow stamens, keeping with good design guidelines using odd numbers for design elements. Also note that the balloons are pulled tightly to give a very smooth appearance. The stamens are simply 260 balloons inflated with a puff of air.

Visit www.balloonstoryteller.com for more information about ACME.

Close-up of one flower

Note: Buster, Annie's husband, made the bride's gown out of 260 balloons.
www.BusterBalloon.com

Photos courtesy of balloonstoryteller.com

Wedding Flower Arrangement

This arrangement is composed entirely of flowers made by stretching balloons over wire frames. Only the foliage is real - even the columns are made from balloons! This creation was designed as a buffet arrangement for a wedding.

Editors note: I didn't know the columns were balloons, too, until Chris pointed it out to me. Wow!

Designer: Christopher Horne CBA - Professional Balloon Decorations, Northampton, England.

A Camellia made with 5" pearl white balloons and pastel green leaves makes a good boutonnière, or good flowers in a bouquet when made with 11" balloons. Make the leaves separately or use silk flower leaves.

This white camellia is made with 11" white balloons. Use these for larger bouquets or group three together for a centerpiece.

Add helium balloons attached to a water or sand-filled matching color balloon weight in the center of three wired camellias for a centerpiece arrangement..

Ideas for Fantasy Balloon Wedding Flowers

Fantasy balloon flowers can be made ahead of time and stored in the dark wrapped in plastic until the day of the ceremony. This will save you time during the days leading up to the event. Make the flowers months in advance if you wish, getting the technique down first before making the flowers for wedding décor.

Below are some ideas for fantasy wedding flowers:

- Bridal bouquet
- Bridesmaids bouquets
- Throw-away bouquet
- Corsages
- Boutonnieres
- Cake Topper
- Buffet Arrangement
- Centerpieces
- Accents for the dance floor canopy or columns
- Bridesmaids headpieces
- Decorate a birdcage, mailbox, or wishing well
- Aisle flowers at the ceremony
- Ceremony décor on top of columns or on candelabra

▶ *Tip: Fantasy flowers last a long time if you keep them in plastic to protect the latex balloons from oxidizing. Designs can be made way in advance, and used over and over again!*

Valentine's Day Flowers

This hanging heart has six different flowers on it. Two have no wire inside (the top and bottom flowers), and the rest are wired 5" flowers with different centers. Wired pink squiggles and silk leaves finish the look.

The heart was purchased at a local hobby store already wrapped with red heart garland. You can find wire frames in any shape at your local floral wholesaler and wrap them with different types of garland for any occasion.

Cut off the necks of 5" balloons. Attach the balloons together with binding wire to make a small flower. Use different colors of balloons as desired.

> ▶ *Hint: Make wreaths for any occasion or season using fantasy flowers and purchased wire frame in any shape*

This flower is made with two colors of 5" latex balloons that are un-inflated with no wire inside. The lip ends were cut off before taping together at the base. Be sure to tape after each petal is attached in order to keep them firmly in place.

Three 5" balloon petals with stamens made from 130 balloon neck ends. Use silk flower or balloon flower leaves.

The three-petal flower above has a center made from a 5" folded balloon with no wire inside and a touch of tulle. This would also make a great boutonniere.

This flower was made in the same manner with the petals closed instead of open and would make a good boutonniere.

Heart Flower and Standing Hearts

I experimented with making wired heart-shaped petals, and found that by bending an 18 or 16 gauge wire into an "M" shape, you could cover it with a heart-shaped 11" balloon and come up with a heart-shaped petal. The petals can be pointed to make a flower, or rounded to make a heart.

Instructions:

1. Pull an 11" heart balloon over an "M" shaped wire and secure with binding wire. Pull both sides of the petals out to form the desired shape, then bend the petals back.

2. For the center, I put a puff of air into a 5" balloon and tied the balloon, then secured it to one of the petals with floral tape.

3. Put two petals together with floral tape to form a flower.

Note the top petal in the photo below. It is more rounded like a real heart shape. This "petal" may also be used as a design element by itself in an arrangement.

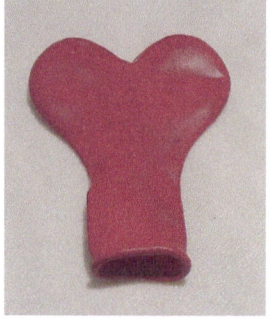
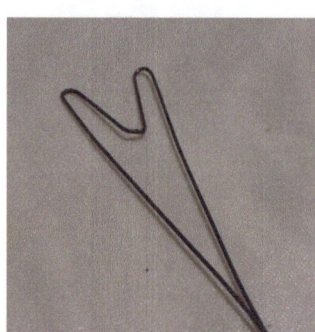
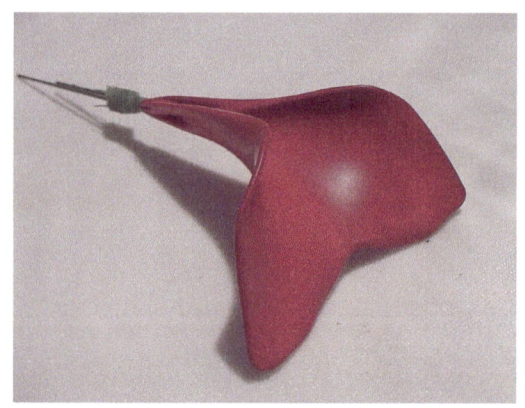

Flower center made by blowing a puff of air in a 5" balloon

Retail and Decor Flowers

11" Balloon flowers in real clay pots with a little moss are a great seller! The center of this flower is just a folded 11" balloon. Add some heart stickers to a plain flower and you've got a Valentine.

Make lots of plain flowers for Mother's day ahead of time if you have a retail store and you'll sell dozens!

These are also perfect for centerpieces for garden parties or ladies luncheons.

Always add leaves—they are the finishing touch to any flower. Make the leaves with more pointed ends so they appear more realistic.

Having a Groovy 60's-70's Theme party? Make these tiny 5" balloon corsages and add a flat center by inserting a small brass ring (available at hobby stores in many sizes) into a 5" balloon. This one uses five balloons, but you could easily add a sixth balloon to make it fuller.

Stretch a smiley face balloon over it if desired. Use small flowers for corsages, and make 11" and 16" balloons for décor pieces. They make great "Flower Power" décor!

Back of flower to show construction.

The Three-Color Flower

The three-color flower is a good item to use in themed events such as Mexican or Italian with green, white, and red; or Fourth of July with red, white and blue.

Instructions: This flower was made with 16" latex balloons. Use orange or yellow stamens made from 260 balloons. For a Valentine theme, make six flower petals using pink, white, and red latex balloons. Instead of overlapping the flower petals, place them so they just meet each other at the sides. Wrap the first three petals together in this manner with floral tape.

Now add petals to the outside of the inner petals, overlapping as you go. Add two green leaves. This is the best method to use when using three colors of petals. Use different color petals if the flowers will be used in a different theme.

Create a different look just by moving the petals around. If an open flower look is desired, you may want to add more petals.

Note how the leaves are pointed and the petals are more rounded.

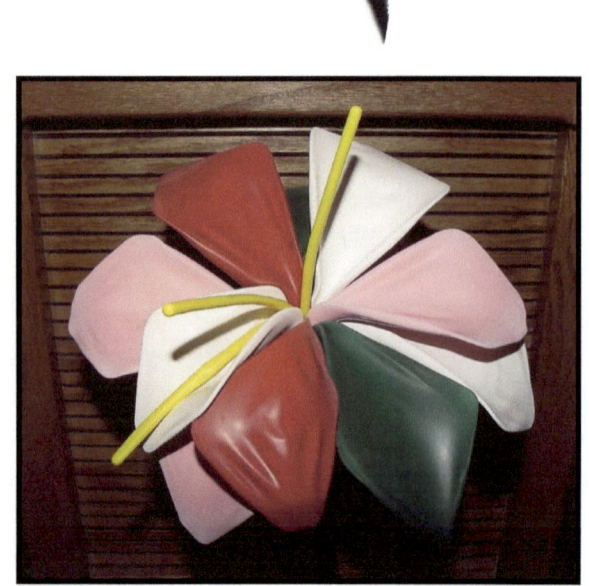

Poinsettia Wreath:

Maggie Brusa used a gold wicker wreath and sheer ribbon like the *Qualatex® Angel Sheer collection.*

The poinsettia is constructed using three 5" red balloons in the center, then two groups of 11" red balloons. The center is made from tiny pearls (sold with wedding supplies), then each group of three balloons was attached using floral tape. Silk leaves were attached with floral tape to the outside.

Poinsettia Sleigh:

The wooden sleigh was purchased from a floral supplier, already decorated with the holly leaves. Maggie filled the sleigh with styrofoam, and covered it with Spanish moss. The candle is held in place with a couple of pieces of floral wire glued into the foam, then pushed into the candle. The centers of these poinsettias are several small plastic "berries", with a dab of gold glitter on each one.

There are two sizes of poinsettias. The first, on the front of the sleigh, was made the same as the one on the wreath. The smaller ones, on either side, were made with six 5" red balloons, taped onto the berry center in groups of 3. The poinsettias were glued into the foam and bent to the proper positions. Any gaps were then filled with pinecones and silk holly leaves.

Courtesy Maggie Brusa, CBA
The Balloon Platoon, Worcester, MA

More Wired Flowers

Stand Alone

Left:
This orange color wired flower has a bead center with shredded balloon stamens, glittered edges on the petals, multiple balloon lips below the flowers to hide construction, and a twisted long wire covered in floral tape to stand the flower on a table. No flower pot needed!

Right:
This peach color wired flower has five petals and a curled unopened petal in the center, and two green wired leaves underneath the petals.

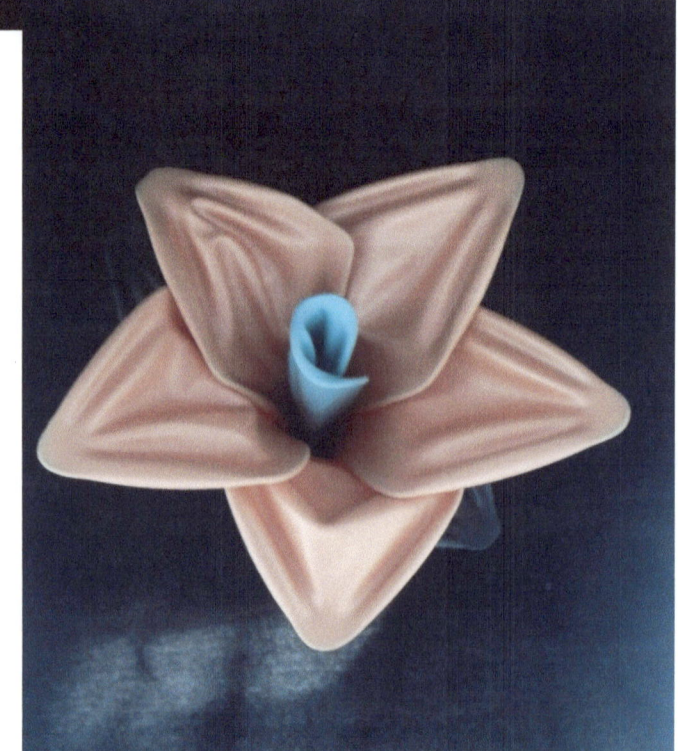

Above: a elegant flower made with three petals and one center curled unopened petal, with one leaf on the side. It is better to use only one leaf with smaller flowers, keeping the elements in proportion.

Right: A 6-petal flower with a center stamen that is not curved. It is made by simply bending a wire and covering it with a tightly pulled 11" balloon.

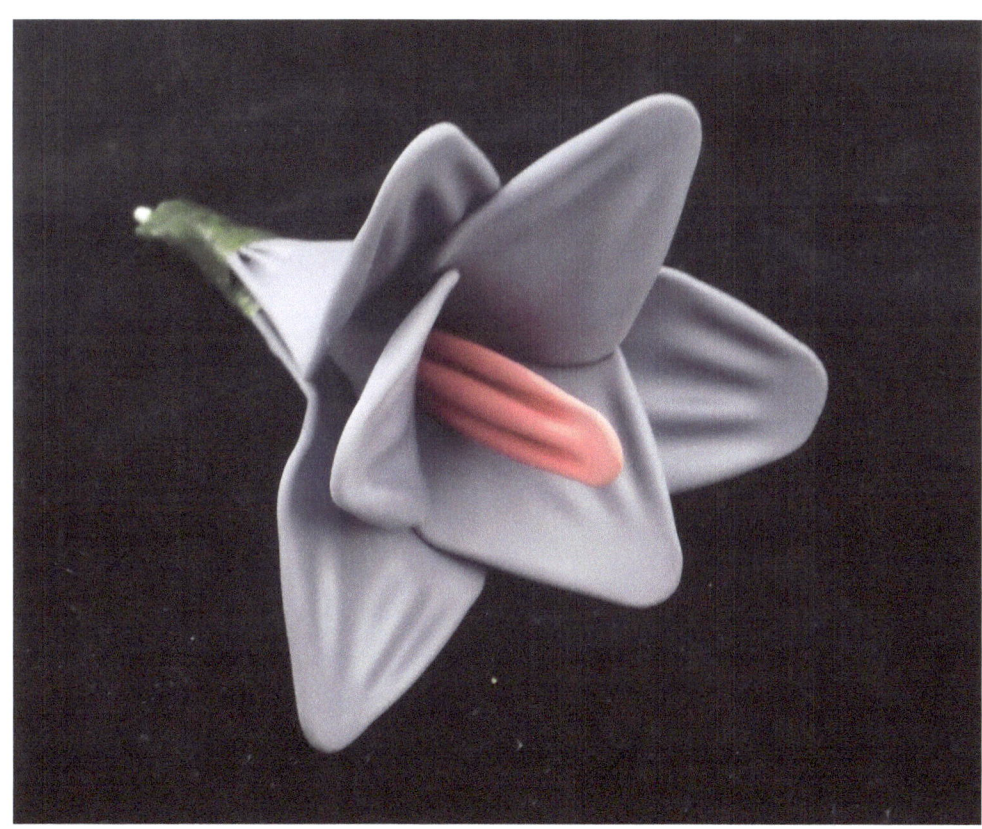

Squiggles and Such

The addition of extra features will make your designs stand out. Be sure to use them in your fantasy flower arrangements. Here are a few ideas to get you started.

Recipe for Balloon Squiggles:

Step 1. Bend an 18 ga. wire at the end with needle-nose pliers. Wrap the end with floral tape so the sharp edge does not poke through the balloon.

Step #2: Pull a 260 balloon over the wire just enough to stretch it, then secure to the wire with floral tape.

Step #3: Wrap the wire around something round such as a permanent marker, pencil, or dowel rod to make the squiggle. Attach directly to flowers with floral tape or insert in an arrangement.

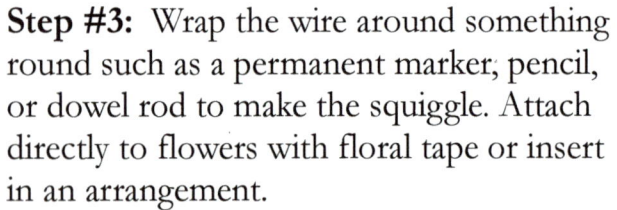
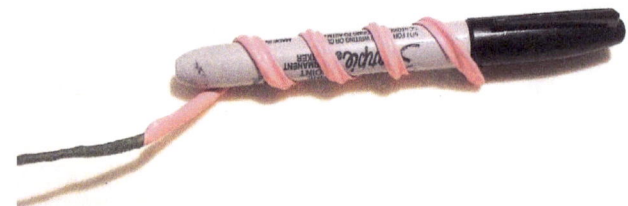
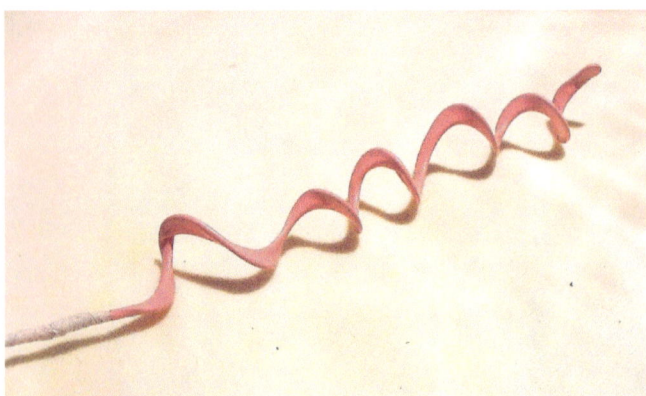
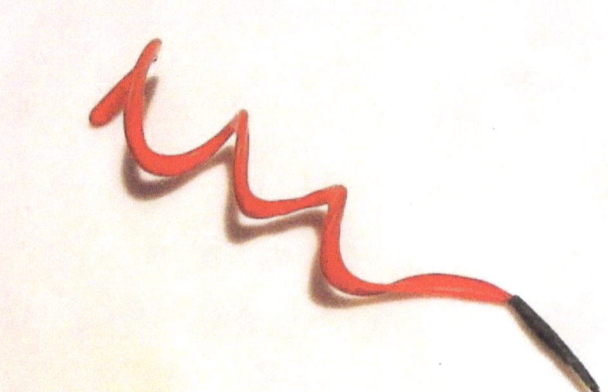

More Extra Touches

- Make simple, fast vine squiggles by wrapping green paper-covered wire around a round object. (no balloons needed)

- Use pre-made silk vines from a craft store.

- Make your own vines by hand by making green fantasy flower leaves and wrapping them one at a time, evenly spaced onto a long floral wire, covering the entire wire with floral tape as you go.

- Add tulle, silk fabric, or ribbons

- Balloon loops (see below)

Balloon Loops:

I like to use these in bouquets, but they can be added to any arrangement. Simply pull a balloon over a wire as in the squiggles, then bend the wire around and secure the two ends together with floral tape. Simple!

Balloon Sticks:

Using the same method as the squiggle, only don't wrap the wire around anything—just leave the wire and balloon straight. Good for larger arrangements where you want to add a splash of color. Use your imagination!

Balloon Flowers and Figures

Leaves are an important part of any floral design. I wouldn't make an arrangement flowers without them.

Experiment with rounded leaves and pointed leaves using round balloons over wire.

Make thin tall leaves by bending an 18 gauge wire in half, then pull a 350 balloon over it and pull the wires out so the balloon is flat. Bend over into a curve if desired. These are especially good for use with Iris.

And silk flower leaves are available in every type imaginable, and can be used along with your balloon flowers as a a quick and easy filler.

 *Design Tip:*

I like to combine different textures and elements in designs. It makes your work interesting, and draws extra attention to the balloon work. If everything is made out of balloons, they don't stand out as much. Try adding silk leaves and ivy, green moss, Spanish moss, real wood sticks, and other elements such as lights, candles, ribbons, and fabric to your designs.

Section II

Fantasy Balloon Figures

Introduction

The fantasy balloon figure idea came to me one night in a dream just two nights before a contest in 1998 in Kansas City, MO sponsored by the KC Professional Balloon Artist's Association. The them was "Fairy Tales," and I had my buffet piece nearly completed. The dream changed my plan, and I had to scramble to get materials for the new design. The funny thing about this is that I never had a love for making fantasy flowers (with wire and uninflated balloons), and it was a big joke around my studio. So when I unveiled this new method for using wire and balloons my staff was shocked.

The first design I made was a woodland scene with one fairy sitting by the water's edge, and another fairy looking down on her from a perch in a tree. I still think that is one of my best designs. From that beginning, the method has been used by balloon artists all over the world, who have created tiny brides and grooms, Samurai soldiers, and circus characters.

I sold my business in 1999 and decided to write a book about the fantasy people method so others could learn how to create miniature designs for their clients. I hope you enjoy making them as much as I have!

Sincerely,

Margie Padgitt

Supplies and Tools Needed for Fantasy Balloon Figures

Most of the tools and supplies needed for making fantasy fairies and people are on a smaller scale that what you might be used to. Balloon artists typically use framework consisting of 1/2" to 3/4' diameter conduit or pipe, agricultural netting, and other supplies that will not be used here.

Making smaller designs requires a change in habit with construction. After a while, you'll get used to the detailed work required to make these small creations.

We'll start with small designs and work up to larger ones. The end product will be determined by the size of balloons you start with.

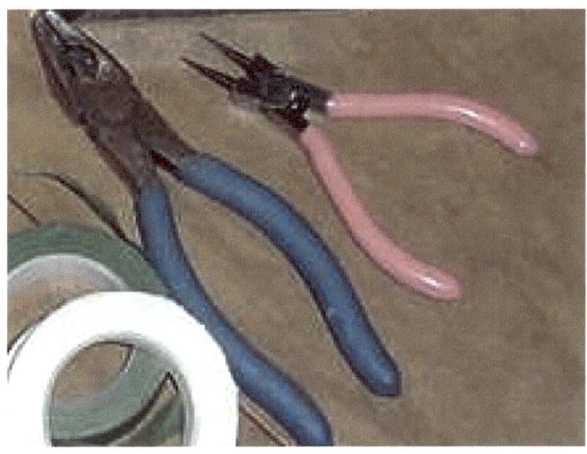

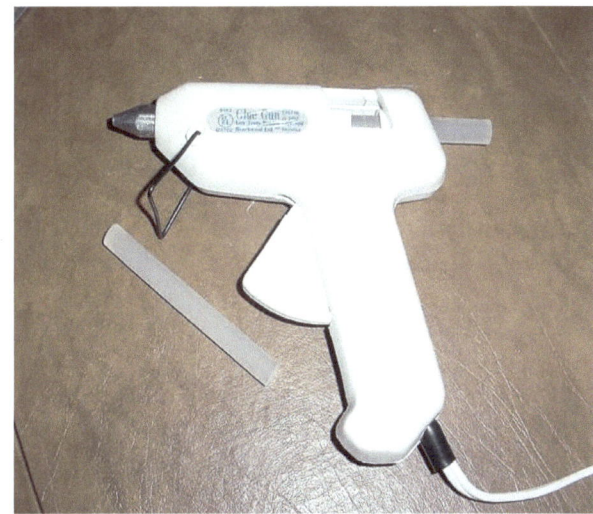

Tools needed to make Fantasy Figures:

- Large and small scissors (sharp)
- Small nail scissors (sharp)
- Small Styrofoam balls or package of assorted wood balls
  (these will be used for heads)
- Tiny needle-nose pliers
- Regular size needle-nose pliers
- Round end pliers
- Wire cutters
- Medium-low temperature glue gun
- Hand balloon pump
- Safety glasses

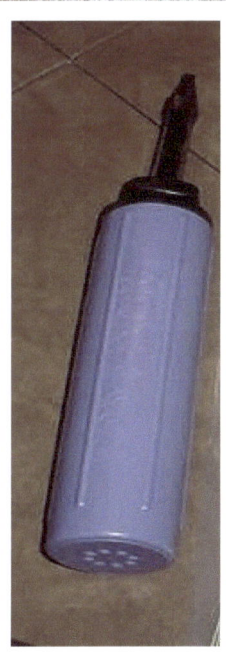

Balloon Flowers and Figures

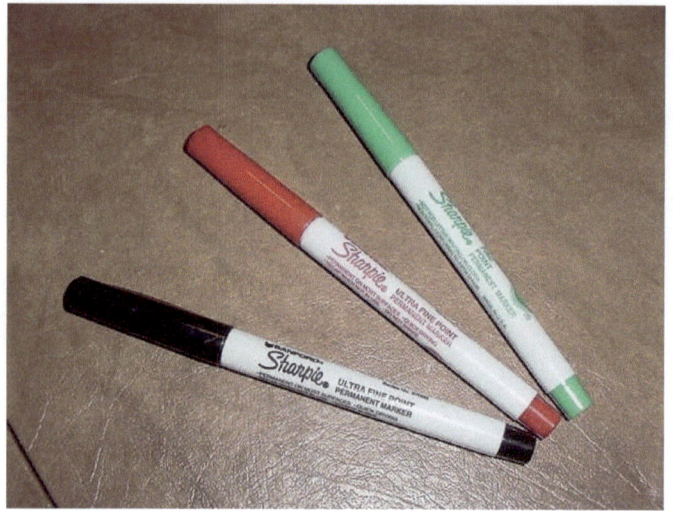

Sharpie brand pens are best for use on balloons because they do not break down latex. Available at most office supply stores.

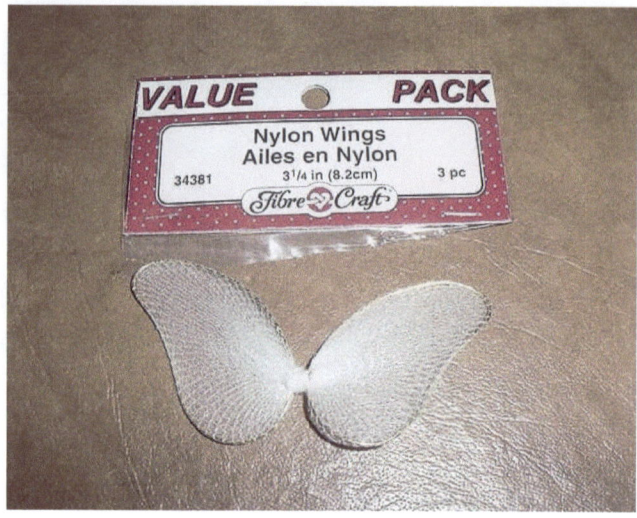

Wings can come pre-made in a variety of styles and save time. Alternatively, you can make your own (see instructions)

Right: Wrap-around safety glasses are a must to use when cutting wire. Bits of wire can fly up very quickly and damage your eyes.

Don't forget to add little extras to your design like frogs, turtles, butterflies and shells or tiny flowers that may be found in a woodland setting.

Supplies such as these can be found at Hobby Lobby, JoAnn's, or similar stores. For larger designs, you might be able to make these extra touches out of balloons.

Supplies Needed

- 18 and 16 gauge floral wire in 18" lengths (Note, wire size gets smaller as the gauge gets larger)

- Green and white floral tape

- Small package of assorted wooden beads (these will be used for heads)

- Rubber cement

- Super Glue

- Sharpie brand small tip markers (for faces)

- Good quality 5", 11", and 16" balloons

- Good quality 130, 260 and 350 balloons (animal or entertainer balloons)

- Balloon ribbons

- Fabric ribbons

- Fabrics and tulle or net

- Thread

- Monofilament line in 5 & 10-lb test (available at fishing stores)

- Other supplies as desired

The Method

The order of construction is very important.
Remember to put your figures together in this order:

1. Build head
2. Construct each arm and leg
3. Wrap legs and arms together
4. Attach head
5. Attach wings (if using wings)
6. Attach clothing
7. Attach hair and head gear

STEP 1—THE HEAD

You'll need peach colored balloons for the faces, arms and legs, but don't be afraid to use green or brown, too.. After all, these are fantasy fairies, elves, and whatever else your imagination can conjure up, so skin color should be whatever suits the design.

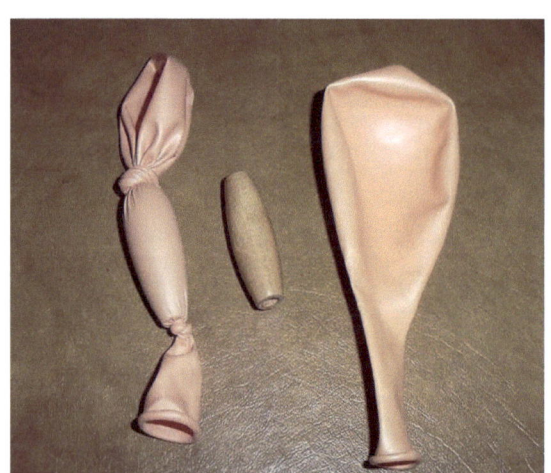

Head method 1:

Stuff a round or oval wooden bead with a hole in the center inside 5" or 11" balloon for the head. If using an 11" balloon, tie a knot at the top of the balloon to make a ready-made turban as seen at the left—so the addition of hair will not be necessary.

To make the head sturdier, bend a floral wire in half and squeeze the wire 1/2" from the bent end. Push the bent end through the bead, then bend the looped end of the wire down around the top of the bead

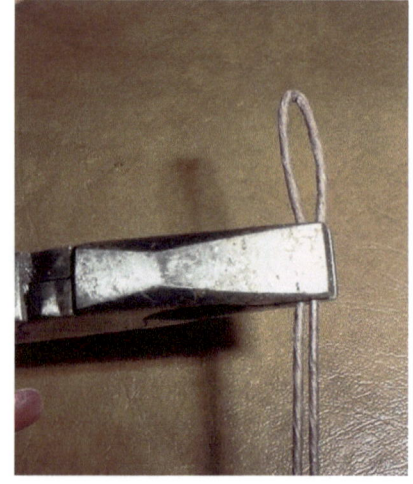

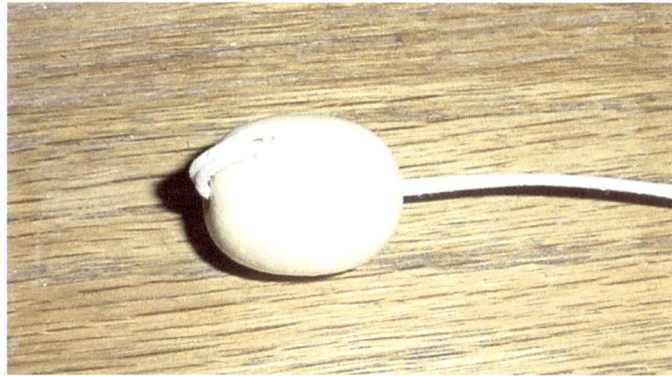

Left: Bead head with wire bent over the top to hold it in place

Left: Bead head covered in a 5" balloon stretched over it, then wrapped with white floral tape to secure it to the wire.

Head Method #2:

Just blow a puff of air into a 5" or 11" balloon, depending on the size of fairy or person you are making. Make sure there is enough air to make the balloon very tight, but not enough to inflate it. Tie a knot close to the air and push the knot down so it is tight, and cut off the lip of the balloon, but leave the rest of the neck.

I prefer not to put faces on this type of head, but experiment and see what you like. You may try putting only eyes on your faces.

Head method #3:

Pick up a small doll head at any hobby store such as Ben Franklin. These heads are very inexpensive and come in a variety of skin and hair color. They are a quick and easy way to add detail to your balloon doll. The heads usually have a wire attached that is long enough to use to support the finished doll.

STEP 2—ARMS AND LEGS

1. Bend an 18" length of 18 or 16 gauge floral wire in half over round nose pliers.

2. Crimp the wire 1/2" from the end. Widen the open end by inserting the round wire pliers and spreading them.

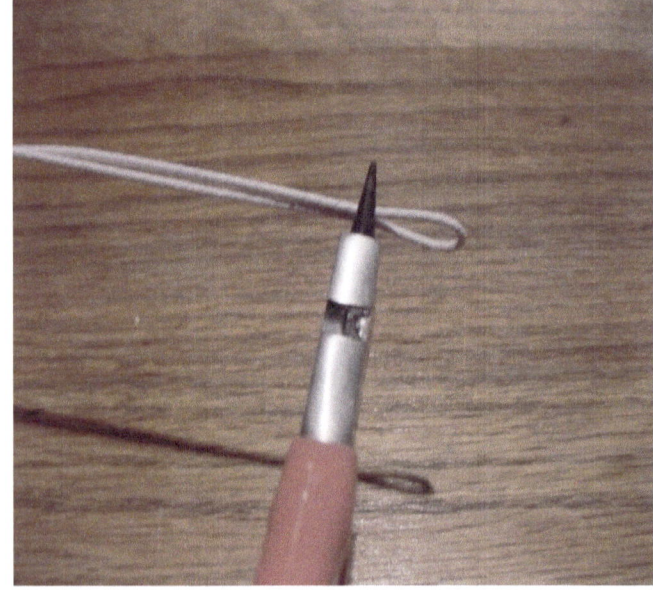

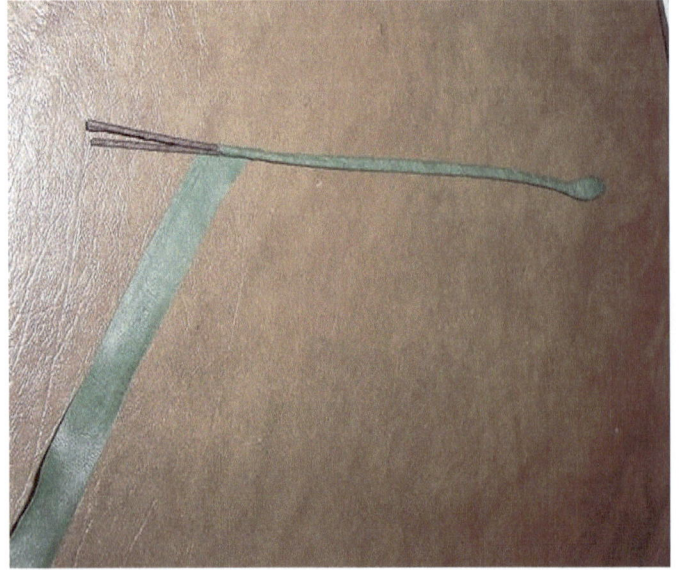

3. Wrap the length of wire with floral tape to 2" before the end, and repeat to make three more arms and legs. If covering in dark clothing use green tape, but if using light colored clothing use white tape.

4. Pull a 260 size balloon in your choice of flesh color tightly over the wires, and wrap the end with floral tape to keep it on the wire. If the balloon is too long for the wire, cut it to length.

Note: If you want your figure to wear tights, use a different color for the legs.

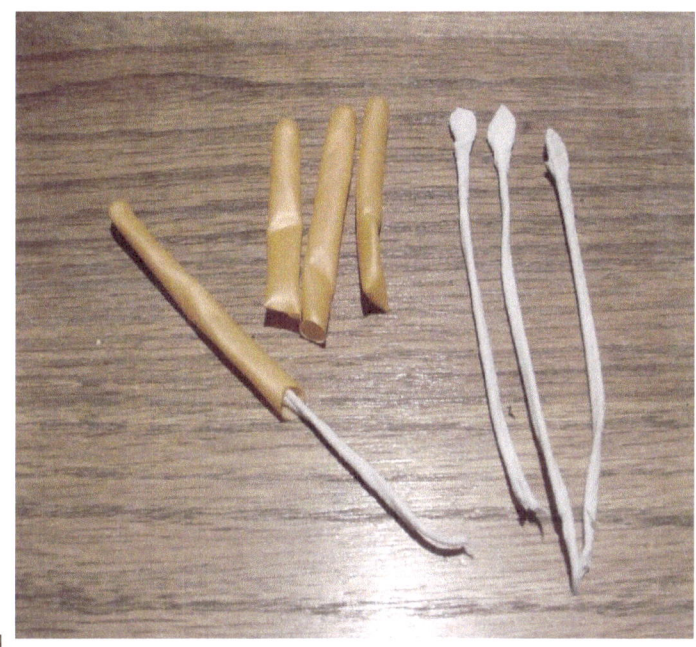

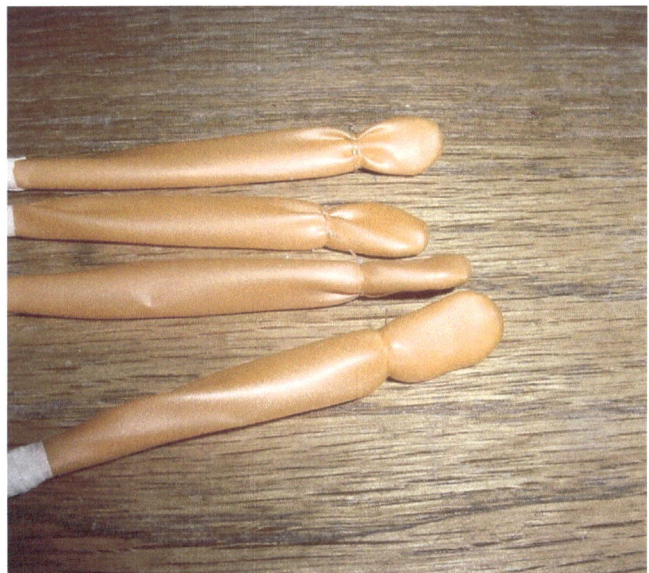

5. .Tie a small cut piece of matching balloon color or 10-lb. Monofilament (fishing line found at Wal-Mart or bait stores) around the ankles and hands formed by the loop in the wires. This defines the shape.

6. To attach the legs, put two wires side by side, and twist the tops together at the open wire ends.

7. Now pull the wires apart, then back together again if desired to make "hips". This step is not required.

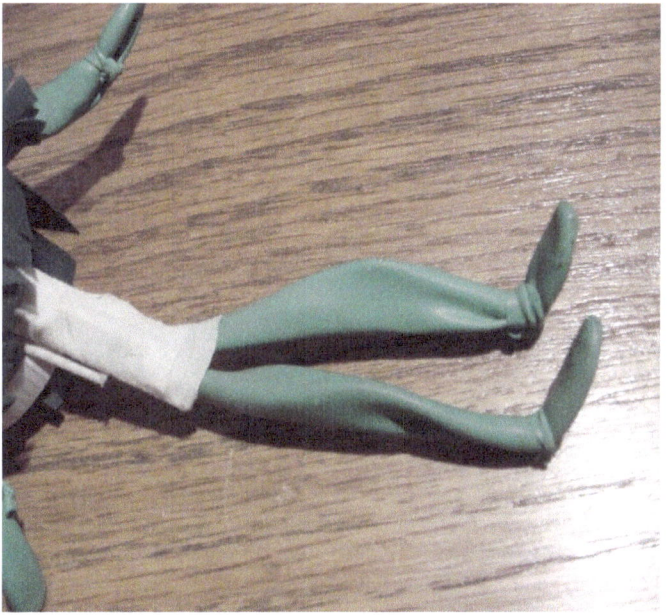

Finishing the Body

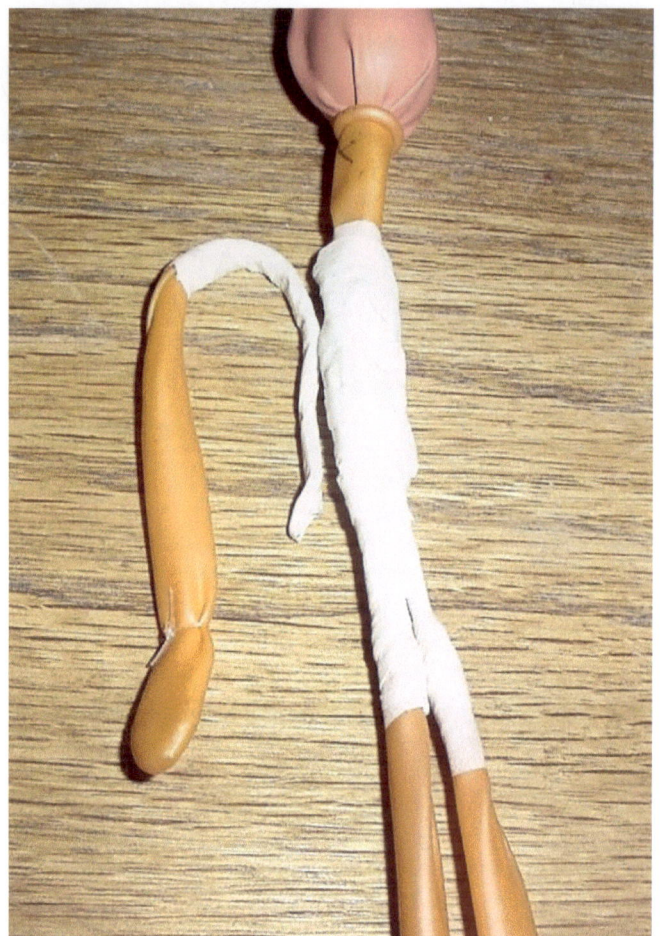

8. Put the remaining two wires side by side and measure for arm length. Cut the wires if necessary, and twist the tops together at the open wire ends. Bend the wire down about 3/4" away to make shoulders, and then bend the arms down.

9. Attach the head by pulling the neck end of the balloon on the head down tight between the shoulders, then wrap onto the body with floral tape. To make a bigger body (for tight-fitting clothing only), add a small piece of filler foam or gauze found at any craft store, and wrap with floral tape to cover it.

10. Attach the arms with floral tape. Now you have a standard body that can be dressed as you please to make a fairy or other character. Remember to make the legs a different color than the arms and head if you want your creation to look like it is wearing tights, or cover the arms in a second balloon to make sleeves, leaving the hand exposed. Pull a 260 balloon over the arm with the lip end at the wrist to make a finished look.

Hint: For a child's party, make a balloon figure to closely match the child's hair, skin color, and clothing. Place the figure on top of a cake or centerpiece to make their day extra special. The child can play with the "doll" for some time.

Fairy Wings

Either used purchased wings from a hobby store or make your own. I have found several different wing styles at Ben Franklin, JoAnn, Michaels, and Hobby Lobby, varying in size from 2" - 9". It is easier to use pre-made wings, but you can vary the look if you make your own.

To make your own wings:

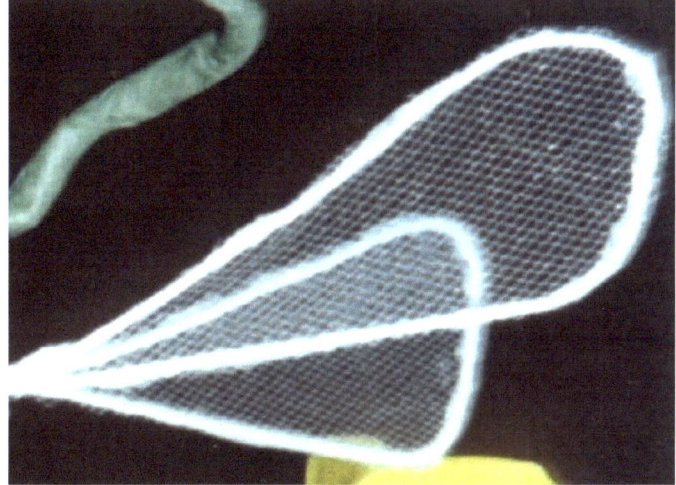

1. use two pieces of white cloth-covered 18" floral wire. Bend the wire in half, then shape into a wing shape. Wings can be single, double (as in a dragon-fly shape), pointed, or rounded. When you have the desired shape, wrap the wire at the base to keep the wing shape.

2. Cut white or other color fine tulle (use bridal tulle—not thick netting) using the wing as a template. Some tulle has a shiny sheen to it—and is very appropriate for use with a fairy. If desired, spray the wings with glitter glue and sprinkle white sparkly dust on them.

3. Using rubber cement or medium-temp glue, glue the netting onto one side of each wing. Trim off any excess tulle.

4. Now put both wings together and wrap with white floral tape. Place the wings onto the back of the fairy in the desired location, and wrap with floral wire to put in place BEFORE putting on the clothing. You will put clothing on around and over the wires attached to the body in order to hide them.

When using purchased wings, just tape them on the body with floral tape or use floral wire, then cover with tape.

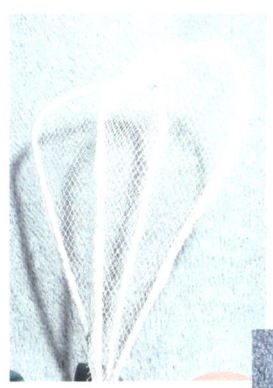

Make handmade wings out of wire and tulle when store-bought won't do.

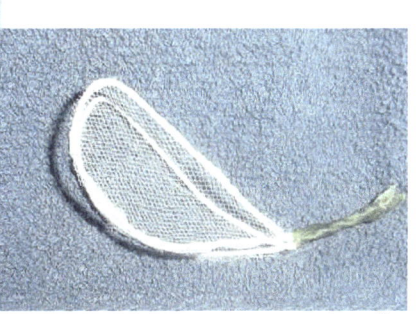

Use white feathers for wings on an angel

Making Clothing

You are limited only by your imagination when it comes to clothing.

To make a simple and fast dress or tunic, take a 16", 18", or 24" balloon and cut off the entire neck. Cut out a half-circle for the head at the top, and cut both sides of the balloon up to the point where you think the sleeve should end. Cut sideways into the balloon to form the sleeve.

Make short cuts in the bottom edge to make a jagged edge. Cut a slit in the back from the bottom to the head opening. Place the balloon on the body, then glue the side edges together to close the tunic. Glue the tunic over the back and around the wings, making adjustments as necessary. If you don't want to use a latex balloon, try using fabric for a different look. Add a balloon or ribbon belt if desired. This style can be used for boy or girl fairies and elves.

To make a **Layered dress,** such as the one the fairy is wearing on the next page—starting with the sleeves, cut the necks off of two 5" balloons. Cut a hole just big enough in the very top of the balloon to fit it over the arm. This may stay in place as it is, but glue the bottom if desired. Now cut 1/2 of the necks of approximately 15 5" balloons, matching the sleeve color. Starting at the bottom of the dress, glue balloons necks onto the body. *Note: Do Not add any air to the balloons)* Continue adding balloons to the body, placing the balloons right next to each other to form a complete circle around the body frame. For the next layer, place a balloon on the body so that the bottom of the balloon covers the

Patterns to cut out of large latex balloons:

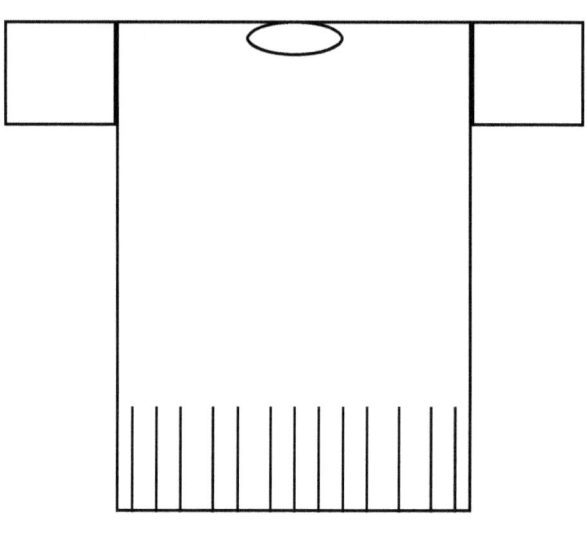

Front

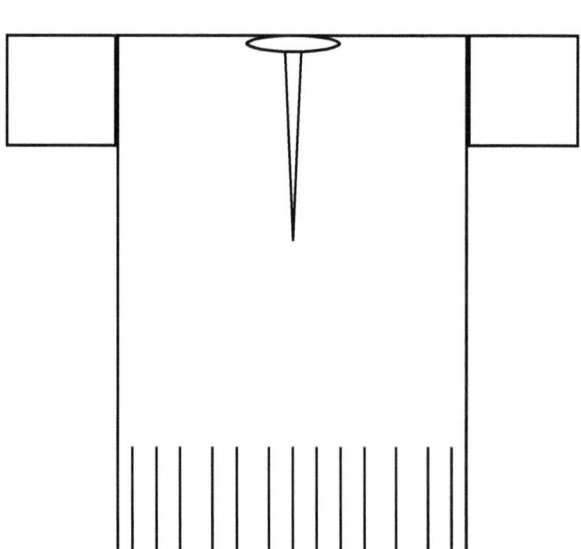

Back with slit cut from neck past wings

neck of the balloon and overlaps to the desired length and fullness. Continue in a circle, and finish layering up to the neck of the fairy. Now cut a 5" or 9" balloon neck off, a half-circle for the head and neck, and a slit up the back and sides. Place on the body just as in method #1, gluing the sides and back. This will cover your mechanics and finish off the dress. Use other materials such as silk leaves for your dress for a more rustic woodland look.

Other materials may be used such as fabric, silk leaves, and tulle for clothing, depending on the event and the look you want to achieve. Use the pattern style here to cut out a simple fabric tunic.

Clothing Samples

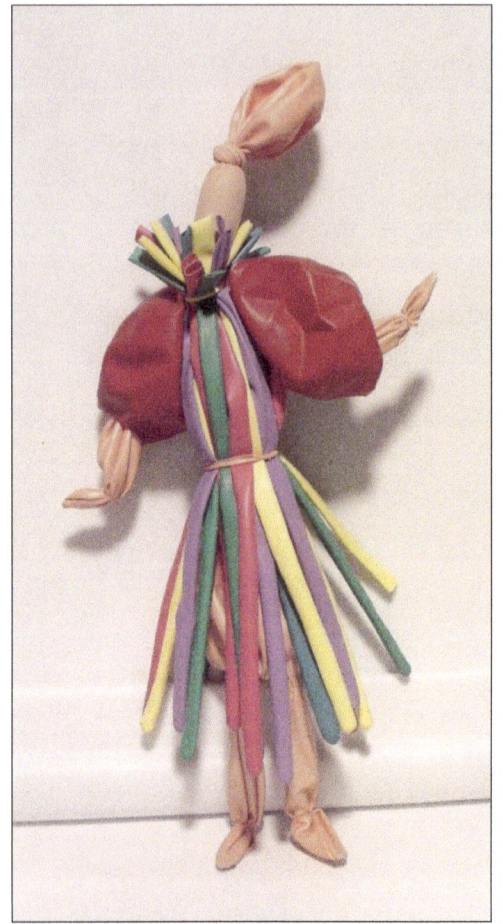

Jamaican Lady's Dress

This Jamaican lady is dancing in her bright colored dress made of uninflated 260 size balloons. The balloons are that are held onto the body by one 11" balloon lip at the waist and one 5" balloon lip at the neck.. This dress is easier to put on if you have someone to help.

1. Lay out the balloons on a table, then gather and hold just above the waist and put on the first lip.
2. Pull the balloons up over the head and pull the 5" lip down over the head.
3. Cut balloons to desired length for the collar. Add two 5", 9" or 11" balloon sleeves and a sash made out of a 260 remnant. Add a face with a sharpie pen if desired.
4. Put one 11" or 16" balloon with the top cut out over the body at the wasit down to just above the skirt hem. This covers the mechanics underneath and makes the skirt flare out.

▶ *Hint: Save all of the balloon pieces that you cut off during construction and use them later for small parts.*

The addition of a sash finishes off the look of the dress. (right)

The larger body figure was obtained by adding several layers of cheesecloth and wrapping it with floral tape.

Clothing for Elves

This girl elf has green arms, legs, and face, with a short piece of a balloon neck pulled up to the bottom of the head with the lip end up. This serves as the neck.
Pull an 11" balloon over the legs and all the way to the top of the arms.

Cut the bottom of the balloon with scissors to make a frayed bottom. Add two 5" balloon sleeves and cut to fray. Glue at the top to hold sleeves on the body.

Make a tunic for a boy elf out of a larger balloon.

▶ *Tip: Bend arms and legs, hands and feet in different directions to give your Fantasy people personality.*

Balloon Flowers and Figures

Fabric Clothing

Clothing may be made out of wired ribbon wrapped around the body and secured with a piece of fabric around the waist, such as the dress at the left.

If you want to spend a little more time, clothing made out of scrap pieces of material can be made, or you may even find small doll-size ready made clothing at a toy store.

Gather the waist with needle and thread, or secure with a rubber band and cover with a ribbon. I like to work with wired ribbon because it conforms easily to the shape desired.

This fairy's dress was made out of one 12" piece of 5" wide wired ribbon.

(Right) A couple of layers of cheese cloth or muslin forms the underskirt when using sheer fabric or wired ribbon.

Left: To make a figure stand up or lean, or appear to be flying, add a piece of wrapped wire to the body at the back with floral tape before adding clothing. Bend the wire at a 90-degree angle to act as a support.

Right: Detail of dress front. Bend wired ribbon to make a front bodice and back, and raise the back up to form a high collar. Leave the neck wrapped in floral tape if desired, or cover with a piece of matching ribbon.

Note that the elbows are toed with matching color pieces of balloons and the wrists are tied with monofilament secured with a drop of crazy glue.

Balloon Figure Hair

Hair can be made out of balloons, ribbon, straw flower petals, raffia, dried Spanish moss, or doll hair. Some figures look good with no hair.

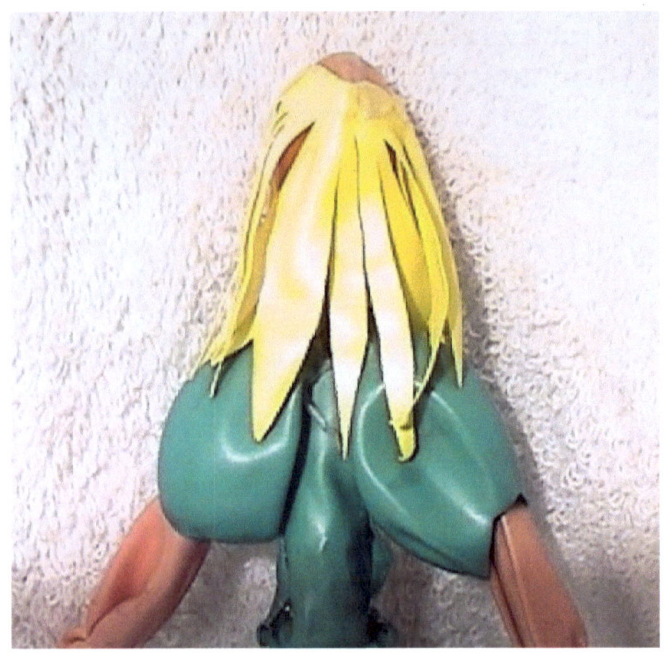

Balloon hair:
This piece of 1 1/2" wide x 2" long yellow balloon was cut into strips, then finished of at the ends with points. I like this style for wild woodland fairies. Simply glue the balloon strip at the top of the head and cover with a hat.

Ribbon hair:
To make ribbon hair, cut 3"-4" lengths of ribbon (or longer, if desired), curl ribbon tightly for the top layers, and loosely for the bottom layers. Glue on the head with rubber cement until the desired look is achieved. Cover with a tiny hat.

This hat is a 5" balloon with the neck cut off, and is glued on with rubber cement. Ribbon hair is lightweight, and good for fairy heads that are made with a 5" balloon with a puff of air inside like this one.

Hats and Headgear

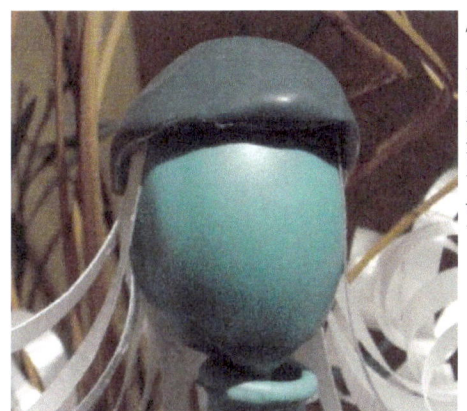

The finishing touch for most of these small creations will be a hat of some sort in order to hide the mechanics of hair, or just to give your figure personality. If using a bead head, a heavier hat can be used, but if using a balloon with air only, you will have to limit the weight of the hat.

The simple cap at the left is just a 5" balloon with the neck cut off. Rubber cement the open end of the balloon, then apply to the top of the head with rubber cement.

Several different looks can be achieved with one hat style. This one is made with a 9" length of wire bent in half, then covered with a 5" latex balloon. Stretch the balloon and wrap with floral tape. Cut the wire to desired length, and then cover with green floral tape again, making sure to cover the end. (Right)

All of these different styles were achieved using the same hat.

Balloon Flowers and Figures

Hats and Headgear, Continued...

The Jamaican lady has a built-in hat when a 16" peach balloon is stretched over a bead head and tied closely to the bead.

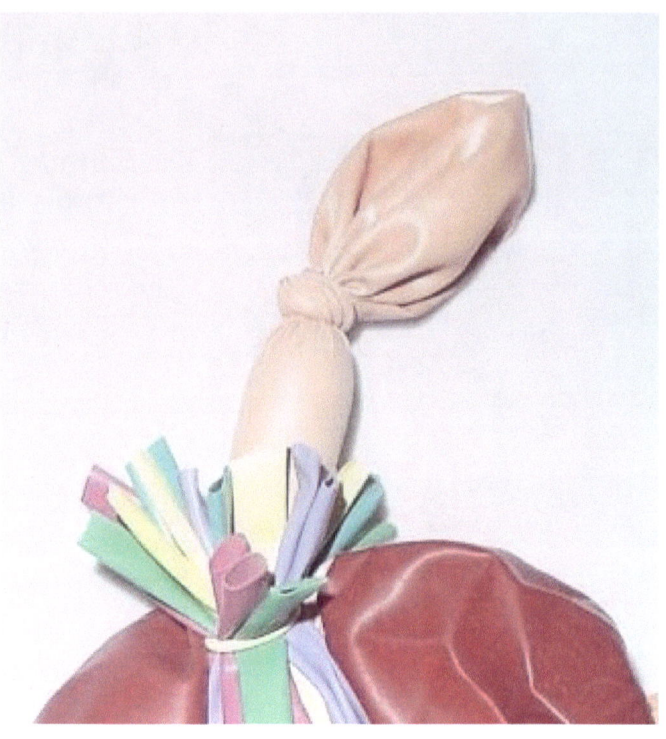

The angel's halo is a wire covered with a 260 balloon and glued at both ends. The rest of the wire is bent down and covered in white floral tape, then cool-glued into the wings and back. (Left)

This crown was formed with silver and gold covered pipe cleaners and glued on with cool glue. (Right)

Petal Dress Doll

This tiny balloon doll was designed and made by my sister, Alice Brink, who is an artist and realtor in Denver, Colorado. Alice had no prior training in this method when she made this figure.

Alice made three 11" petals with very wide rounded wire inside for the base of the dress, then added a 5' petal for the apron. The head is a bead head that is not covered with a balloon, and has doll hair. The arms and sleeves were made in one step with one piece of bent wire covered with two 11" balloons (meeting in the center), then wrapped around the body wire. An inflated 5" balloon makes her dress top. The figure is supported by the petal dress so no wire support is needed.

The tiny wood butterfly is a great touch. You can find these at hobby stores.

The nice thing about this type of design is that you there is no need to make legs or feet so it cuts down on construction time.

Fairy with Petal Dress

Using the piece of clip-art shown here from www.clipart.com, lets make a fairy petal dress like this one. Note that many fairies you see in books appear to be wearing flowers, petals and leaves. This fairy has flower stamens for a crown.

Recipe:

1. Make a basic body, but cover the legs in yellow or orange balloons instead of peach so it looks like the fairy is wearing tights.

2. Make five petals out of 16" orange or pink balloons. Make sure to form a point at the end of the wire before inserting it into the balloon.

3. Bend wires down just above the floral tape on each petal so that no tape shows. Attach all 5 balloons to the body with floral tape (you may have to bend the petals up first). Bend petals down.

4. attach a matching color balloon underneath the petals to cover the body.

5. Cut two 5" balloons for sleeves, making points like those in the picture. Glue on pieces of balloons cut into points to finish off the neck.

6. Cover the feet with a short piece of a 260 balloon that has been cut at an angle to look like a boot. Tie monofilament line at the ankle to hold it in place, then bend the foot to the angle desired. Add tiny leaves with rubber cement.

7. Add desired hair and cap or silk flower stamens.

A Woodland Elf

This charming woodland elf is surprisingly fast and easy to make, and uses just three balloons for the clothing.

Using a standard body, cover in green latex 260 balloons for the arms and legs, except bring the toes to a point when bending the wire for the feet. Use a bead head or air head out of a 5" green latex balloon.

For the dress, use one 11" dark green balloon, and two 5" dark green balloons for the sleeves. Cut the sleeves and dress bottoms with sharp scissors approximately 1/4" apart.

Add hair of your choice and a small green cap, or make the cap with wire and make a pointed cap. Bend the pointed toes slightly upward if desired.

Purchase small props from a miniature shop, toy store, or hobby store to create the setting for your tiny people.

The above design was made with a styrofoam base covered with green moss attached with greening pins, and dried leaves and curled stems inserted directly into the base. You would want to add some color in the form of flowers, butterflies, or bugs to this design. Also be sure to place some color behind the green elf, such as a yellow flower, so the elf stands out better. This design can be easily modified to make a boy elf.

A Balloon Ballerina

This ballerina can be made in about 20 minutes. Start with a standard body, but don't bend the feet—you'll want her to stand on her toes.

Instructions:

1. Make a standard figure body and use the head type of your choice.

2. Cut an 11" balloon at the neck, thread the balloon over the legs and onto the body to make the underdress, and then pull the cut neck over the dress and up to the shoulders. Glue both balloons in place with rubber cement. If desired, make some shoulder straps out of strips of balloons and glue them in place under the balloon neck.

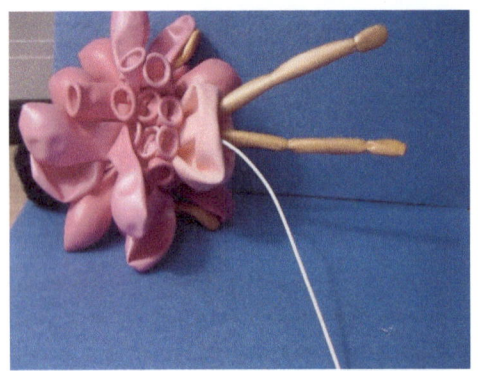

3. I used the wire from the head purchased at Ben Franklin, wrapped it into the body with floral tape, and used it to make a stand so the figure would stand up by itself.

4. To make this balloon tutu, simply lay 5" latex balloons onto the waist with the neck end down. Tie around the waist with monofilament line about 1/2" above the end of the balloon neck, then pull the balloons over the top of the monofilament so they are facing down ward. Use two or three layers for a full tutu.

To make a net tutu, cut stiff netting (not bridal tulle—it is too soft) into strips 3" - 4" wide and approximately 12" long. I used 8 layers here. Thread on a wire, pull the netting to gather. Attach to the waist, then twist the wire in the back.

Or, using needle and thread or monofilament, sew 1/4" from the edge, gather, attach to the doll and sew the back together.

Same balloon doll— different tu-tu's

Note that I did not bend the feet out but left them straight so it would look more like a ballerina on point. A small end piece of a balloon could be added for toe shoes.

Fantasy Balloon Angel

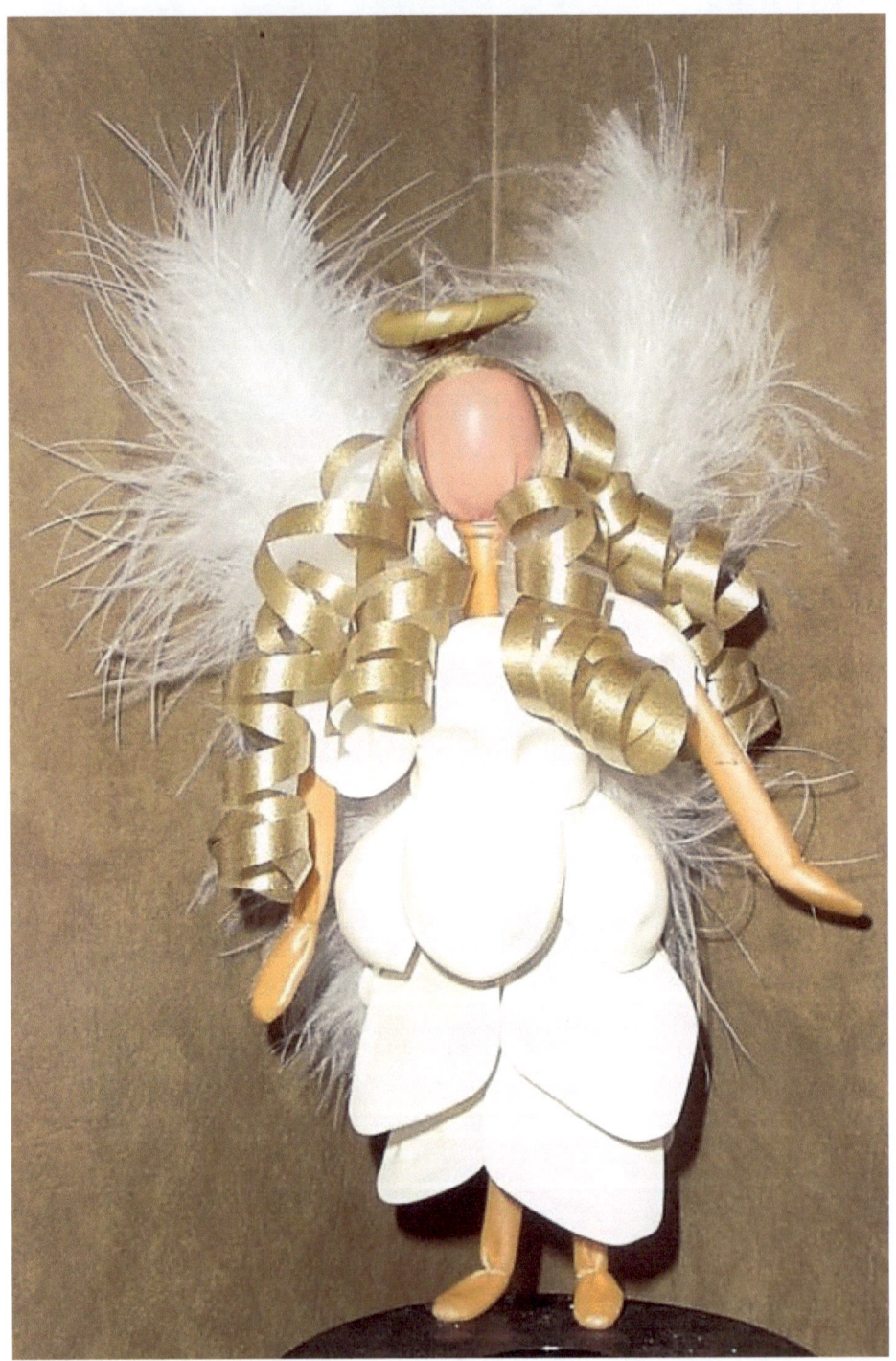

Since angels are very popular and the reader may find that they are in high demand, I decided to build one step-by-step so you can see the entire process. This takes a little longer than most small figures do, so be sure to charge more for it. Estimated time to construct: 1 hour or more.

Use as Christmas ornaments, gifts, or holiday table décor.

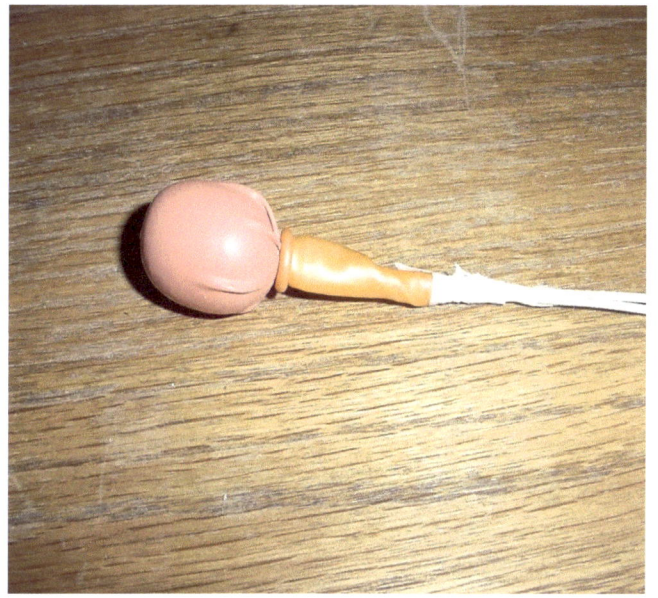

1. Make a bead head with wire as on page 12, and wrap the stem tightly over the balloon neck just underneath the bead with white floral tape. Cut a 1" piece off of a peach 260 balloon and insert over the wire with the lip end towards the head.

2. Make arms and legs as described in the method, then wrap legs together with floral tape.

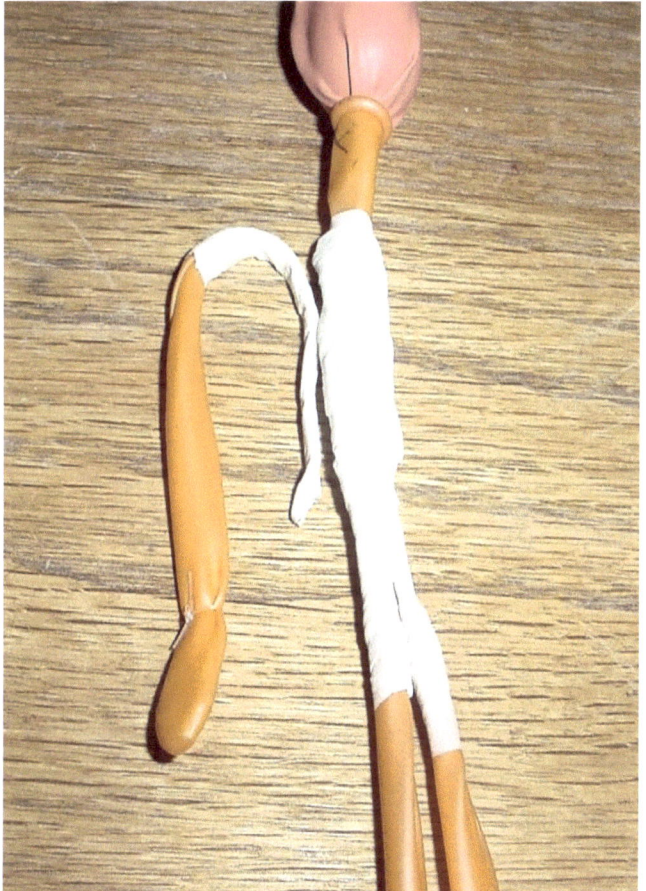

3. Add head by attaching head wire to leg wires with floral tape.

4. Attach arms. Measure arm length, bend to form shoulder. Make second arm before attaching first arm in order to keep the length the same. Attach both arms with white floral tape. You may want to bend the arms up and out of the way to make it easier to attach the arms.

5. Make eight dress petals. Cut the lip ends off of 5" round balloons. Then, bend a 9" piece of wire in half and insert into a 5" round white balloon. Pull the balloon down onto the wire, and while holding, cover the end of the balloon and wire with white floral tape. This is a little tricky. Just remember to pull and stretch the floral tape so it will stick. Wrap a second time to make it more secure if desired.

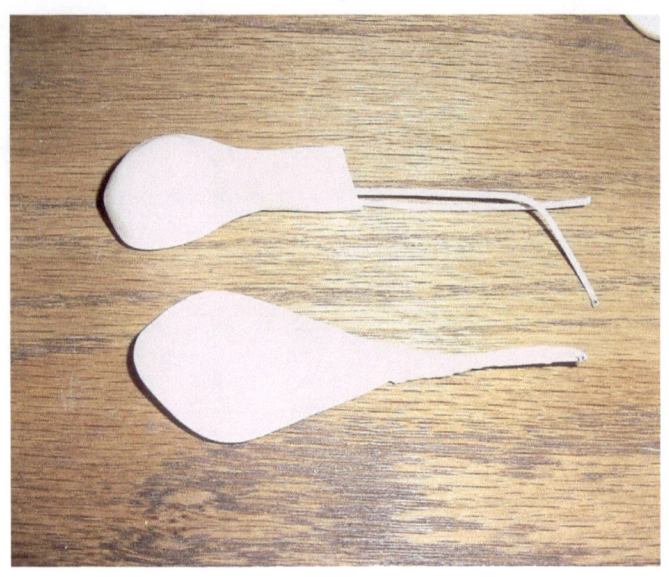

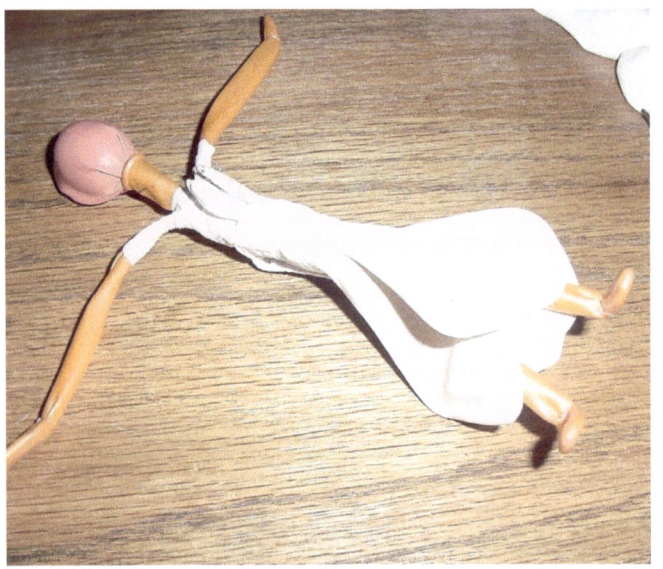

6. Attach bottom layer of petals by holding all of the petals together in the center, then wrap with floral tape. Make sure each petal overlaps the one next to it. Dress length is up to you.

7. Add second layer of petals over the first, making sure that mechanics are covered. You will have to trim wires from the ends of this row of petals, or bend them down to form the body of the angel. Wrap tightly with white floral tape.

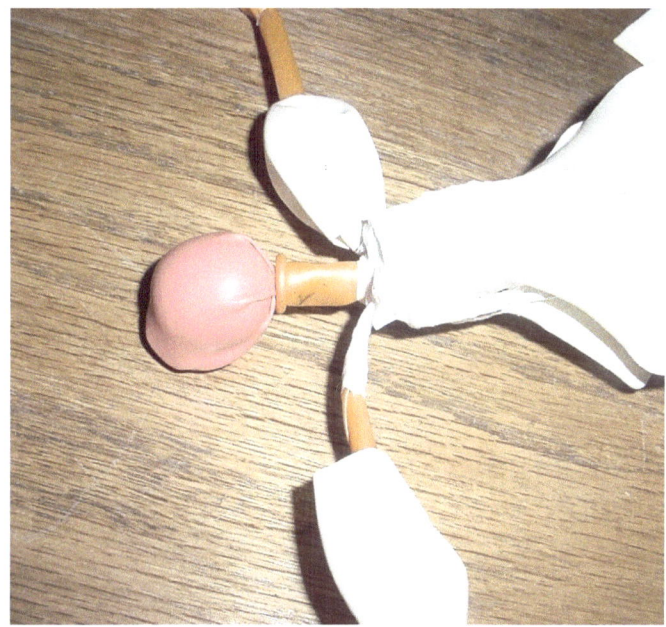

8. Add sleeves. Cut the necks off of two 5" round white balloons, and cut a hole in the top end of each balloon. Thread onto arms, and attach the top part to the shoulders with rubber cement.

9. Wings. Attach store-purchased wings with monofilament line. Wrap the center part of the wing with monofilament first, then run one end over a shoulder, and the other underneath a top dress petal and tie in front. This way, the wings will stay centered. This is the base for the feathers.

10. Finish dress. Cut 5" white balloon necks off, and attach to the torso by wrapping with white floral tape. This step is done after the wings are attached. Glue all or part of a balloon in front to cover the tape.

11. Bodice. Cut the entire neck off of one 5" round white balloon, then glue upside down onto the top of the dress to make the bodice. Cover mechanics by wrapping the center with a sash made out of a white 260 balloon and glue in back with rubber cement.

Balloon Flowers and Figures

12. Feathered Wings: Cut feathers to length desired, then glue one white feather on each side of the top part of the wings, and glue one feather on each side of the bottom part of the wings, using a total of eight feathers. Be sure to place all feathers so they are bending to the back.

13. Hair. Curl gold or yellow ribbons to desired length. Attach 4 or 5 ribbons to the top of the head. Shred ribbons if desired, and curl tightly. Or use doll hair or gold mylar.

14. Halo. Wrap the 4" center part of a 9" length of fabric-wrapped wire with a gold 260 balloon in a spiral fashion, and glue at each end. Pull the wire around in a circle to form a halo, and bend wires down for the stem. Wrap the stem tightly with white floral tape, then glue the halo on the back of the head and body with cool glue.

Add a face with a sharpie pen if desired— or just a mouth or eyes. I prefer not to draw faces on my creations.

Left: Finished back

Circus Figures

These great Circus Figures were designed and created by Johnna Perry of Up Up and Away Balloons and Entertainment in Liberty, Missouri for a contest.

Johnna made a ringmaster, clown with balloons, an acrobat, lion tamer, and of course, a ferocious lion. All out of latex balloons, wire, and air.

Note: The circus tent was made with 160 balloons inflated with air.

Ringmaster

Clown with balloons held up with wire

Balloon Flowers and Figures

Lion:
Air inflated balloons and wire provided the base for latex balloons covering the parts of this lion. Put a puff of air inside a small 5" balloon and tie off, trip the neck, and push inside an 11" or 16" balloon, put a dime inside of one of the 5" balloons to make a flat top for the forehead. Make a mouth out of two wired petals, and glue this onto the face. Use uninflated 130 balloons for the mane. Flat toothpicks covered with balloons were used for the teeth. Glue a pink 130 balloon inside the mouth for the tongue. Glue 130 balloon lip ends on for eyes and nose. Standard wired legs were used here. You may also place a piece of Styrofoam inside a balloon to make a body, then insert the wired legs and tail through the balloon into the Styrofoam.

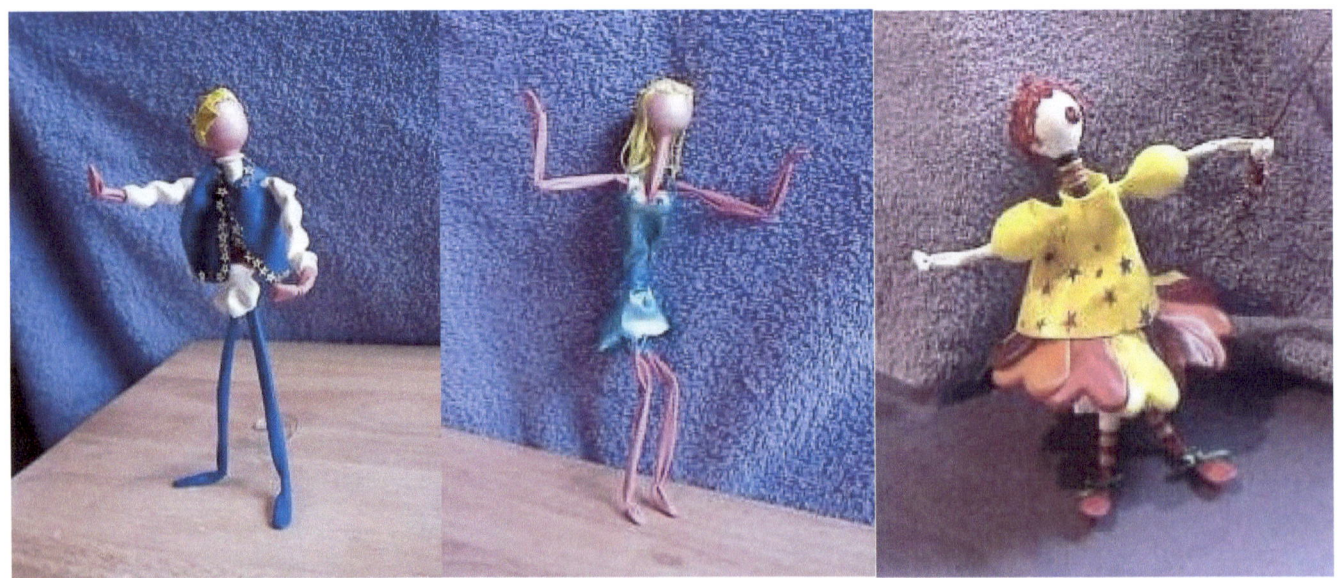

Lion tamer   Acrobat   Clown

The clowns stockings and neck covering are balloon lips cut off the ends of small balloons. The hair for these figures is made from shredded latex balloons.

Balloon Clown

Using the same techniques described below, my friend Johnna Perry, of *Up, Up and Away Balloons* in Liberty, Missouri made this cute girl clown. She was created using longer and wider wire framing for the feet. The legs and neck are covered in multi-colors of cut-off rolled tips from 360 balloons, the underskirt is made from 5" white round balloons and the overskirt is made from multi-colored heart shaped balloons. The hat has not yet been added in these photos.

Ingredients:

Assorted 5" heart balloons
White 5" balloons
Two yellow 5" balloons
Four white 260 balloons for arms and legs
Two red 260 balloons for feet
Assorted 130 or 260 balloons for lip ends
Monofilament line
Rubber cement
18 ga wire
White floral tape

Instructions:

1. Cut an 18" length of 18 gauge wire in half.

2. Bend wire in half with needle nose pliers or electricians pliers (these are perfectly round)

3. Pinch wires together 1/2" from bent end for hands, and 3/4" for feet.

4. Insert a cut flesh color 260 balloon over the bent end, pull slightly, then tape with floral tape at the base.

5. Bend the rounded end of the wire to form a hand or foot and tie thin monofilament line over the wrists, elbows, and ankles. Add the neck ends of 260 balloons to the legs to make striped socks.

6. Make another of each of these and floral tape together to form the legs and feet.

7. For the head: put a wooden bead with a hole in the center over a piece of wire. Bend the wire down over the bead about 1" or less. Add floral tape underneath the end that is not bent to secure the bead to the wire. Add enough tape to build up the neck.

8. Cut the neck ends off of several 260 balloons and insert them over the wire at the base if the head. This is the neck.

9. Attach the bead head on the wire to the legs, measuring to see that it is proportioned to form the head, body and legs. Cut off excess wire and attach with floral tape.

10. Attach each arm separately, bend at elbow and wrists and tie 3 lb. monofilament (fishing line) over these places to make them more de-

Balloon Flowers and Figures

fined.

11. Make an underskirt by wiring uninflated white balloons on the body, then add the overskirt using 5" heart balloons. Cut the necks off of two 5" balloons and slip then over the arms and glue. Add a top by cutting the top off of a 16" star balloon and cut down the back to open it up, Place over the doll and glue.

12. Add hair made out of balloons (see tip at right) or doll hair and a hat if desired. Add a red 130 lip end nose. Add three 5" air-filled balloons on wires if desired.

Close-up of neck with balloon neck ends covering it.

Clown with underskirt (petticoat)

Clown with overskirt

Photos and design courtesy of Johnna Perry, Up, Up and Away Balloons and Entertainment, Liberty, MO

Finished Clown with 16" balloon bodice, and hair made from curled strips of 360 balloons. The balloons were curled on an 18 gauge. wire, then baked in a 200 degree oven for a few minutes to set the shape.

To make balloons that appear to float put 5" air-inflated balloons on the ends of fabric-wrapped floral wire.

To support the figure, add a third wire to the body when adding the legs, bend this wire to the back, making a tripod.

Sometimes I add a third wire when adding the legs to use for support so the balloon figure stands up by itself.

More Circus and Zoo Figure Ideas:

Zoo habitat (boulders, grass, trees)
Zoo tram or lift
Bears—Elephants
Rhinoceros—Monkeys
Tigers—Panthers—Other large cats
Penguins—Flamingoes—Pelicans
Alligators—Lizards—Snakes

Cycle riders—Acrobats–Trainers
Cannon and man—Clown cars
Stands for animals

And inside the circus tent items that can be made with framing and covered in balloons:

Inside circus ring
Hoops (use rings from craft stores for frames)
Stands for elephants and tigers
Drapes used for acrobatics
High-wires and swings
Cannon
Clown cars
Tricycles and Bicycles

Framing can be made out of many different types of items and covered in inflated or uninflated latex balloons. Use foam core, heavy construction foam, oasis, thin plywood, or chicken wire cut to shape, or make your own frame out of 16 gauge wire.

Bar Mitzvah Figures

These are some very creative ideas for fantasy figures. Sandi Masori, owner of Balloon Utopia in San Diego, California, used the wired balloon figures technique to make one-of-a-kind centerpieces for a Bar Mitzvah with a move theme.

Sandi used balloons for the clothing, doll hair, and a felt top hat for these figures and placed them on old movie film reels..

A Sushi Bar

Sandi Masori designed and created this unique sushi bar by covering a miniature wood counter with latex balloons. She added two figures making sushi and a waitress using standard fantasy figure techniques. Some balloons have wire inside and some are simply cut latex balloons. Sandi opted not to include facial features, which is also my preferred method when creating small figures.

Close-up of sushi chef.

A Balloon Mermaid

What little girl (or big girl for that matter) wouldn't love to have this cute mermaid on top of her birthday cake or in a centerpiece?

Ingredients:
Two blue or green 5" balloons
Two blue or green 360 balloons
Two 260 balloons in flesh color
One 5" flesh color balloon
Bead for head
18 ga wire
Two tiny seashells
Purchased doll hair
Monofilament line
Rubber cement

Instructions:

1. To make the fins, bend wire over a pencil, pull only one side of the wire out, forming a triangular shape.

2. Cover each of the fins with a 5" green or blue balloon with lip end cut off. Tape together with floral tape.

3. Make the arms and head just like the standard fantasy figures, and leave a long piece of wire to attach to the fins. Attach with floral tape.

4. Wrap the body with something to make it bigger, such as cheesecloth or cotton.

5. Wrap the entire body from the fins to the neck in an un-inflated 260 or 350 balloon in a matching or similar color to the fins and secure with rubber cement. Add two tiny seashells for her top and some doll hair.

▶ *Tip: I attached the doll hair with glue dots that are available at most balloon suppliers. Balloon hair may also be used.*

A Balloon Seahorse

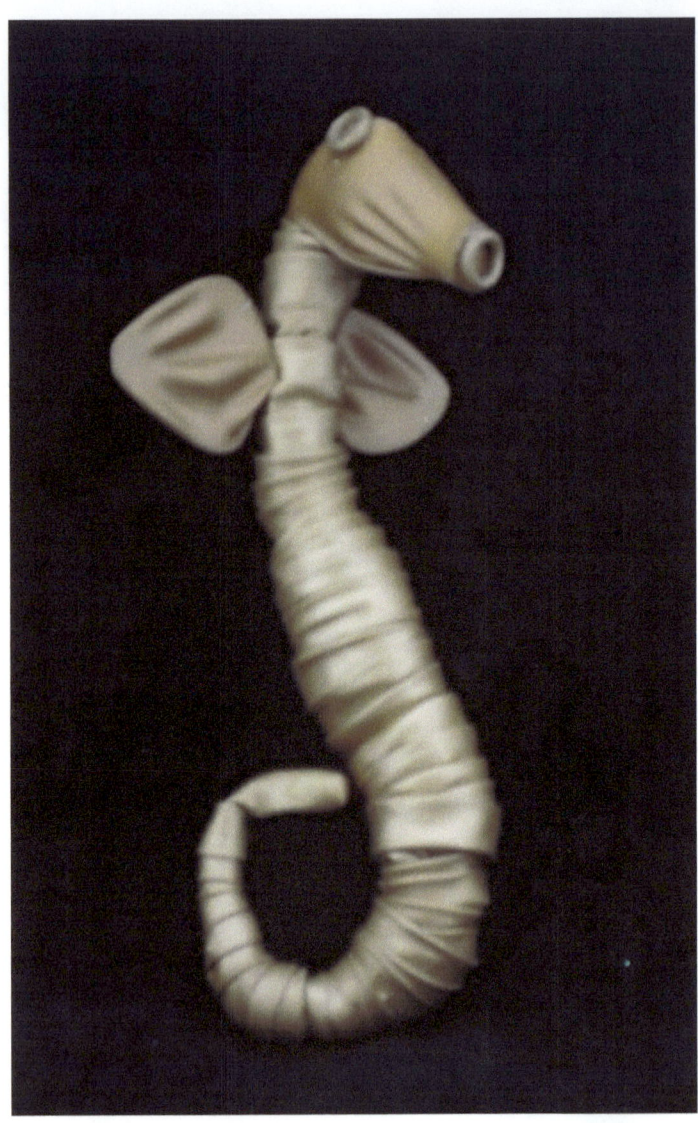

A perfect addition to an undersea theme with the mermaid, this seahorse is easy and fast to make.

Ingredients:
Oblong wooden bead
Three 5" gold balloons
16 and 18 gauge wire
Several 260 gold balloons
Binding wire
Glue
Gauze

Instructions:
1. Bend the tip of a 16 gauge wire over the end of the bead, insert the wire into the bead.
2. Cover the bead with a 5" balloon and stretch it over the wire, then wrap with binding wire. Bend the wire down at a 90 degree angle.
3. Cut the neck ends off of three 260 balloons and glue on the seahorse head for the mouth and eyes.
4. To make fins, bend two short pieces of 18 gauge wire in half, cover with a 5" balloon with the neck cut off close to the top of the neck and bind with wire.
5. Measure and cut a 10" length of 16 gauge wire and wrap with gauze to give the body some shape. Attach the head with floral tape.
6. Start adding 260 balloons with the necks cut off at the neck of the seahorse, then tape on the two fins, and finish covering the body with 260 balloons. Bend the tail up.

Woodland Fairy Centerpiece Arrangement

Ingredients:

- 12" green styrofoam wreath
- 18" round piece of green outdoor carpet
- 4—6" round mirror
- Blue cake gel
- Green silk ivy vine
- Stick from your yard
- 3" round piece of styrofoam
- Three small and one large 3-petal Fantasy Flowers
- Two or three preassembled fantasy balloon fairies
- Greening pins
- Medium-temp glue

Instructions:

1. Cover the round mirror with blue cake gel and set aside to dry for 24 hours.

2. Cover the styrofoam wreath with green outdoor carpet, and attach to the wreath with greening pins. Push the center down to allow for the "pond."

3. Cut a stick to the desired height, cover with medium-temp glue at the bottom, and push into the styrofoam at one side. Push greening pins in around the stick to hold it more securely.

4. Place 3" round piece of styrofoam on the top of the stick, remove, put medium-temp glue on the stick, and replace the styrofoam.

5. Place 11" uninflated balloons around the styrofoam to cover it and attach with greening pins.

6. Attach fairies in positions desired using greening pins around their body or legs where they won't be visible.

7. Glue "pond" in the center of the arrangement. The gel will be sticky, so try not to touch it.

8. Attach flowers and vines.

Fantasy Fairies

These fairies were used in the centerpiece design on the previous page.

To make fairies, use the standard techniques described earlier for the heads, legs and bodies. Add a pair of homemade wings made out of bent wire covered with tulle, gossamer, or balloons and attach the wings to the back of the body with floral tape Add clothing and hat or hair of your choice.

I don't draw on faces but you could do so with a fine-tipped sharpie pen if desired.

Kids and adults love fairies– so you can't go wrong with a fairy theme party! Don't forget to make some boy fairies wearing pants or shorts. A fairy queen or princess is also a must if making a large arrangement.

▶ *Tip: Bend fairies into different positions to add interest to a design. Keep creations in plastic bags when not in use to keep air out—they will last a long time this way and can be used over and over again.*

Figures Made with Balloons and Other Materials

Balloon Flowers and Figures

Purchase wired fabric flowers from craft suppliers and make them into dresses for tiny fairies or people. The flowers (green flower at right) come with a long 16 gauge wire stem.

To make:

1. Turn the flower upside down and bend the petals down to form the dress. Cut the wire to length for the body.
2. Make a wood bead head covered with a 5" balloon.
3. Cover the wire in a small piece of 260 balloon with the neck end up to form the neck of the figure.
4. Add arms covered in 130 balloons, then add two cut pieces of 260 balloons for the dress sleeves.
5. Attach the body to the wire on the flower with binding wire.
6. Wrap the body of the figure with a flat 260 balloon that is glued at the top and bottom to hold it in place,.
7. Add two lip ends of 130 balloons to the wrists to make bracelets.
8. Glue uninflated 5" balloons to the body to form the upper part of the dress, matching the color of the flower.
9. Add hair, hat, and if desired, wings.

Page 118

Where to Use Balloon Flowers and Figures

For Decorators:
- Garden Party
- Tea Party
- Flower, Lawn and Garden Shows
- Easter Designs for Malls or Church plays
- School Plays
- Proms
- Weddings and Special Events
- Conferences
- Spring or Summer themed events
- Grand Openings
- Display for Garden Centers
- Children's Birthday Party
- Party for Adults
- Theme Parties

For Retailers:
- Valentines Day
- Mother's Day
- Holidays
- St. Patrick's Day
- Use for Store Window Displays
- Use to sell any time of the year!
- Banquet table décor
- Centerpieces
- Buffet Arrangements
- Anniversaries

Wired flowers and figures can last a long time if kept sealed in plastic and out of the sun, so they can be used over and over again.

A Lovely Bride

Surprise a bride at her shower, or make a groom to go with it and use them for a wedding cake topper or unique centerpiece. This design would be especially appropriate if balloons are used elsewhere for décor. Make weeks ahead of time and keep in a plastic bag and it will be perfectly fine on the big day.

Ingredients:
Oval bead
16 gauge wire
One white 350 balloon
Two white 130 balloons
Two peach 130 balloons
One peach 260 balloon
One peach 5" balloon
Nine 11" white or pearl white balloons
Doll hair
Small piece of tulle
Glue
White floral tape

Directions:
1. Place wire and bead inside a 5" balloon using technique described earlier.
2. Make two arms-cover with peach 130 balloons, then cover each with a white 130 balloon that has the ends cut off to make sleeves the length desired.
Add a peach balloon for the neck.
3. Wrap the arms together with the wire from the head and neck with floral tape. Do not add legs (they are not needed).
4. Make nine white wired petals.
5. Layer the petals together to form the dress with one longer petal added for a train. Wrap all the petals together and cut wires off at the proper length just below where the neck will be located.
6. Wrap the body with a flat 350 balloon.
7. Glue Doll har on the head.
8. Attach a piece of tulle to the hair for a veil.

If the bride will let you see her wedding gown ahead of time, try to match the gown design as closely as possible. If a longer train is desired, add more petals

with long wire attached
Change the peach balloons out to another color if desired to match the skin color of the bride (and groom if making a doll for him, too).
Add tiny pearls or lace trim purchased at a craft store if desired.

Section III

Resources

Glossary of Terms and "Balloonisms"

These are terms that are specific to the balloon industry and are used in making Fantasy Flowers and Figures

Airhead: Someone who works with balloons all day. Not derogatory.

18-gauge: The most commonly used wire size for wired fantasy flowers, used with 11" balloons.

16-gauge: Wire used for larger flowers with 16" latex balloons.

20-gauge: The smallest wire used with fantasy wired flowers—for 5" balloons only.

260: A balloon that measures 2" wide x 60" long when inflated.

130: A balloon that measures 1" wide x 30" long when inflated.

350: A balloon that measures 3" wide x 50" long when inflated.

CBA (Certified Balloon Artist™): This program, a training and testing course for balloon decorators, is offered by the Qualatex™ Balloon Network and can be purchased at most wholesalers who carry Pioneer Balloon products.

Center: The middle part of a fantasy flower - can be made to look like stamens, or a flat center similar to daisy centers.

Color Wheel: A tool used by designers to help create pleasing combinations of color. Here is a great website where you can purchase a color wheel online: http://www.colorwheelco.com/

Complementary colors: Located opposite each other on the color wheel. Blue, for example, is the complement of orange. Complementary colors enhance each other in decorating schemes.

Fantasy balloon flower: Any type of faux flower or copy of a real flower made out of balloons.

Fantasy fairy: First created by Margie Padgitt, these are tiny fairies and people made with latex balloons and wire, similar to the wired fantasy flower method.

Floral tape: A special tape that when stretched and pulled sticks to itself. Comes in different colors.

Floral wire: A light gauge wire used to secure floral or balloon arrangements together.

Fru Fru: A term used to describe a ruffely ribbon, tuft of tulle, lace, or other element in balloon work that adds a change in texture and highlights the design.

Hue: Color, eg. red, blue or yellow.

Lip End: The rolled, open end of a balloon.

Loop: A loop made out of an animal balloon or wired balloon as part of a fantasy flower or arrangement.

Monochromatic: A color scheme that uses shades and tints of the same color. Example: violet, dark purple, burgundy.

Petal (wired): One petal in a fantasy flower, formed by inserting wire into an un-inflated latex balloon.

Primary Colors: Red, Yellow, and Blue.

Secondary Colors: Violet, Orange, and Green.

Monochromatic: A color scheme that uses shades and tints of the same color. Example: violet, dark purple, burgundy.

Primary Colors: Red, Yellow, and Blue.

Secondary Colors: Violet, Orange, and Green.
Shade: Hue mixed with black.

Sharpie Pen: The Sharpie brand pen is used for work with latex to add details. It will not harm latex balloons like other types of pens.

Size: Means to make all of the balloons in a flower the same size. Use templates, electric balloon sizers or "eyeball" the balloons.

Stamen: The pollen center part of most real flowers. We use fake stamens to add detail to balloon flowers.
Squiggle: The official term for a twisted wire or balloon.

The Balloon Lady (or The Balloon Guy): Your name when you are on a job.

Tint: Hue mixed with white.

Tone: Hue mixed with grey.

Twist: A section of latex balloon that is twisted by hand to pinch off the air in the balloon, and allow another section to be secured to it.

Twister: *Only NON-Twisters don't know this.* It means someone who twists balloons into funny shapes for a living. Also known as balloon entertainers or buskers.

Wired flower: A fantasy flower made with wire and latex balloons.

Wired ribbon: Ribbon that has wire on one or both edges. It can be bent into different shapes more easily than non-wired ribbon.

Wired flower: A fantasy flower made with wire and latex balloons.

Wired ribbon: Ribbon that has wire on one or both sides. It can be bent into different shapes more easily than non-wired ribbon.

Resources

The following are places where I've purchased supplies and materials for making the designs in this book. Check online or on your cell phone for coupons before you go to the store in person or online:

Hobby Lobby (Beads, feathers, tulle, tiny hats)
www.hobbylobby.com

Michaels (Ribbon, wire, doll hair, icing gel, Styrofoam, mirror)
www.michaels.com

Joanne Fabrics & Crafts
(Wire, beads, ribbon, fabric, floral tape, craft items, hand tools)
www.joann.com

True Value Hardware (Tools, wood dowels)
www.truevalue.com

Home Depot (Wood, tools)
www.homedepot.com

Lowe's (Tools, fake grass, glue)
www.lowes.com

Menards (Tools, wire)
www.menards.com

Bass Pro Shop (Monofilament line)
www.basspro.com

Amazon.com (nearly everything is available here, including balloons)

Balloon wholesalers:

American Balloon Factory
Overland Park, KS
800-210-7328
www.americanballoonfactory.com

Loftus International
Salt Lake City, UT
800-453-4879
www.loftus.com

Balloons 'N More
Silver Spring, MD
800-869-6673
www.balloonsnmore.com

More resources can be found in my book "The Balloon Business Kit," 2018, available at amazon.com

Organizations, Social Media, Magazines

Balloon Council
This is an organization formed in 1990 made up of retailers, distributors, and manufacturers that are dedicated to educating others about balloons. They offer a certification for retailers. This site has a lot of information about balloons that you should know. check their website at **http://www.theballooncouncil.org/**
Executive Director
Lorna O'Hara
Princeton House
160 West State Street
Trenton, NJ 08608
Phone (800) 233-8887
Fax (609)989-7491
Email contact@tbc.com

Balloon Artists Forum
on Facebook @balloonartists
Where balloon artists learn and share

Balloon Decorators
Facebook group for photos and discussion about decorating with balloons.

Balloonhq.com
This is a HUGE resource for anyone in the balloon industry. Join to get photos, videos, event calendar, get balloon recipes and add your business to the artist directory, and join the entertainer or decorator forum. www.balloonhq.com

Balloon Professionals Chat List
Hosted by Margie Padgitt. A place to discuss and share techniques and ideas.
https://groups.yahoo.com/neo/groups/BalloonPros

Balloon Magic Magazine
Quarterly magazine published by Qualatex
www.qualatex.com
Also visit their Facebook page

Balloon Images Magazine
www.thequalatexevent.com

Party & Paper Retailer Magazine
www.partypaper.com

Certified Balloon Artist
Get this designation through Qualatex at www.qualatex.com.

Publications by Margie Kithcart-Padgitt

Balloon Flowers and Figures 2018, available at Amazon.com
The Balloon Business Kit, 2018, available at Amazon.com
Supercharge Your Balloon Business! (Marketing audio tape) 2004
The Color Therapy Chart 1996
Creative Use of Color in Business 2000
Marketing Your Service Business 2018
The Chimney and Hearth Professional's Resource Book 2010 & 2016, available at Amazon.com
Homeowner's Guide to Fireplace and Heating Appliance Maintenance and Operation 2018
The Complete Chimney and Fireplace Restoration Manual (in progress)
Documentary film: A History of Chimneys and Chimney Sweeps
Wood-Fired Magazine: Available at www.woodfiredmag.com
The MCSC News Magazine (trade magazine)

And under the pen name Margie Kay:
The Ghost Hunter's Field Guide, available at Amazon.com
Haunted Independence, available at Amazon.com
Un-X News Magazine, available at www..unxnews.com
The Kansas City UFO Flap, 2018, available at Amazon.com

Margie is available to speak at conferences and meetings on business building and industry topics.

Contact:
Margie Padgitt
M. Padgitt & Associates
P.O. Box 1166, Independence, MO 64051
816-833-1602
Fax 816-461-2818

E-mail address: ympadgitt@yahoo.com
or margepadgitt@comcast.net

Website: www.balloonedu.com

About the Author

Margie Kithcart-Padgitt is a popular writer, publisher, and speaker. She hosted two radio shows for seven years, owned and operated a party and balloon decorating company for 19 years, and has been the CEO of a specialty chimney contracting business since 1982. Margie and her husband, Gene, also own a real estate investment company and specialize in restoring historic homes. One site they own is the birthplace of Ginger Rogers, which has been converted to a museum. The Padgitt's employ 19 people.

Margie founded the Kansas City Balloon Artists Association, and served as president and newsletter editor for six years. She has served on national and regional boards of several organizations since 1993.

Padgitt created fantasy balloon figures in 1998 just prior to a contest in Kansas City. She perfected the technique, then taught the method at balloon conventions and meetings. Margie has spoken at multiple regional and national conferences and meetings on various subjects, including balloon décor, business, and marketing.

Margie lives in Independence, Missouri with her husband, Gene, and their cat, patches. She has two children and seven grandchildren.